Glass Bells from Around the World

A. A. Trinidad, Jr.

Glass Bells from Around the World

A. A. Trinidad, Jr.

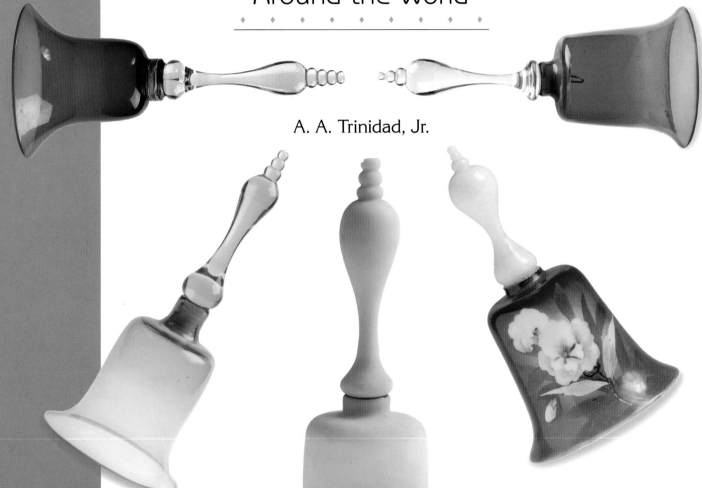

Schiffer Publishing Ltd

4880 Lower Valley Road · Atglen, Pennsylvania 19310

Schiffer Books are available at special discounts for bulk purchases for sales promotions or premiums. Special editions, including personalized covers, corporate imprints, and excerpts can be created in large quantities for special needs. For more information contact the publisher:

Published by Schiffer Publishing Ltd.
4880 Lower Valley Road
Atglen, PA 19310
Phone: (610) 593-1777; Fax: (610) 593-2002
E-mail: Info@schifferbooks.com

For the largest selection of fine reference books on this and related subjects, please visit our web site at **www.schifferbooks.com**
We are always looking for people to write books on new and related subjects. If you have an idea for a book please contact us at the above address.

This book may be purchased from the publisher.
Include $5.00 for shipping.
Please try your bookstore first.
You may write for a free catalog.

In Europe, Schiffer books are distributed by
Bushwood Books
6 Marksbury Ave.
Kew Gardens
Surrey TW9 4JF England
Phone: 44 (0) 20 8392 8585; Fax: 44 (0) 20 8392 9876
E-mail: info@bushwoodbooks.co.uk
Website: www.bushwoodbooks.co.uk

◆　◆　◆　◆　◆　◆　◆　◆　◆　◆　◆　◆　◆　◆　◆

Type set in BenguiatGot Bk BT/Zurich BT

ISBN: 978-0-7643-3488-7
Printed in China

◆　◆　◆　◆　◆　◆　◆　◆　◆　◆　◆　◆　◆　◆　◆　◆　◆　◆

Dedication

To my many bell collector friends at the American Bell Association who have encouraged me to prepare this book on glass bells.

Acknowledgments

The contribution of information from many bell collectors and organizations has made this book possible. My thanks especially to Marilyn Grismere, Mary and Ken Moyer, Sally and Rob Roy, Virginia Wilson Toccalino, The Butler Institute of American Art, The Powerhouse Museum, and Gail Bardhan of the Rakow Research Library at the Corning Museum of Glass, for providing much information.

Contents ◆ ◆ ◆ ◆ ◆ ◆ ◆ ◆ ◆

Introduction   8

Chapter One: Canadian Bells   11

    Chalet Artistic Glass, Ltd.
    Demaine Glass Studio
    Galactic Art Glass Studio, Inc.
    Snookum Art Glass Inc./ Robert Held Art Glass
    Rossi Glass, Inc.

Chapter Two: European Bells   33

Austria 33
    Palda Glas
Belgium 34
    Val St. Lambert
Bohemia 36
Czechoslovakia 37
Czech Republic 37
    Rückl Crystal A/S
Denmark 41
    Holmegaard Glassworks A/S
France 42
    Cristalleries Royales de Champagne (Bayel)
    Cristallerie Daum
West Germany 45
    House of Goebel
    Graf Schaffgottsch'sche Josephinenhutte
    Alfred Taub, Vohenstrauss, GmbH
East Germany 48
    Lausitzer Glashuette, AG
Hungary 49
Ireland 50
    Cavan Crystal Designs, Ltd.
    Failte Crystal
    Galway Irish Crystal, Ltd.
Israel 51
    Jenny Kravits
Italy 52
Norway 63
    Hadeland Glassverk A/S
Poland 63
    Krosno, S. A.
Portugal 64
    Atlantis, S. A.
Romania 65
Serbia 66
Slovakia 66
Slovenia 67
Spain 67
    Vidrios de Arte Gordiola, S.L
Sweden 68
    Ekenas Glasbruk

Mantorp Glasbruk AB
Orrefors Glasbruk
Switzerland 69
United Kingdom 70
Burns Crystal Company
Caithness Glass, Ltd.
Dartington Crystal, Ltd.
James Deakin & Sons, Ltd.
The Edinburgh Crystal Glass Company
Gleneagles Crystal Company, Ltd.
John Gosnell & Company
Mackay & Chisholm
Nazeing Glass Works, Ltd.
Royal Doulton Crystal
Sperrin Crystal
Stevens & Williams
Tudor Crystal Designs, Ltd./Dial Glass Works
Thomas Webb & Sons
Wedgwood Crystal, Ltd.
William Comyns & Sons, Ltd.
English Bells of Unknown Makers
European Bells of Unknown Makers 80

Chapter Three: Asian Bells   85 ◆

China 85
Japan 86
Kagami Crystal Company, Ltd.
Noritake Company, Ltd.
Sasaki Glass Company, Inc.
Taiwan 87
USSR 88
Gus-Khrustalny Crystal Factory
Asian Bells of Unknown Makers 89

Chapter Four: Australian Bells   91 ◆

Melbourne Glass Bottle Works

Chapter Five: South American Bells   93 ◆

Venezuela 93
ICET Art Murano

Chapter Six: Wedding Bells   95 ◆

English Wedding Bells
Butler Institute of American Art

The American Bell Association   159

Index   160

Introduction ♦ ♦ ♦ ♦ ♦ ♦ ♦ ♦

Bells have been used as a means of communication and ornamentation in world cultures for over three thousand years. Generally, bells have been made of metal, porcelain, wood, clay, and glass. Among collectors you will find all types of bells. This book focuses attention on glass bells, presenting them by country of origin, type of glass, and manufacturer when known. When the manufacturer is unknown, the bells are presented as unknown or in a special grouping.

The prices for bells vary based on condition, age, number made, availability, and attractiveness to the collector. Therefore, for bells shown herein, a range of values generally has been shown.

In recent years, many bell producing companies have closed or merged with other companies. The attributions presented in this book are the latest the author has been able to determine. Bells previously shown in the author's books, *Glass Bells* and *Collectible Glass Bells of the World*, are not repeated in this book unless additional information has become available.

The author has gathered photographs from museums and bell collectors for this book. They are shown under the respective countries or producers to which they are attributed. The names of museums and collectors who furnished information are shown when requested or approved.

Canadian Bells

There are many glass companies in Canada and some have produced very artistic glass bells.

A Chalet clear glass bell with ruffled rim and 3 large knops handle. 5.25"dia. x 8.5"h. $60-75.

Chalet Artistic Glass, Ltd.
Cornwall, 1962-1975

Chalet Artistic Glass was founded by Angelo Tedesco, a glass cutter from Murano, who invited other glass cutters and blowers from Murano to Canada. The bells that were produced sometimes have the name Riekes also on the label. Riekes is a wholesale distributor who for over fifty years has imported glass products from Asia, Europe, Canada, and South America.

Demaine Glass Studio
Mactaqac, New Brunswick, 1975-1980

Martin Demaine made a limited amount of glass bells over a short period of time. His bells are distinct in their decoration.

Two Demaine glass bells. The left bell is clear light blue glass with cream colored swirls. Signed "Demaine '77". 3.1"dia. x 7.25"h. The bell on the right is dark clear blue with white decoration. Signed "Demaine Studios '76". 4.1"dia. x 8.25"h. $75-85 each. *Courtesy of Sally and Rob Roy.*

A Demaine clear glass bell on the left with blue ribbon decoration and a blue snake wrapped around the handle. Signed "002 Demaine '76". 4"dia. x 7.25"h. The Demaine bell on the right has a gold-brown base with clear glass protrusions on the clear glass round handle. Signed "Demaine Studios '78". 3.4"dia. x 9"h. $75-85 each. *Courtesy of Sally and Rob Roy.*

Galactic Art Glass Studio, Inc.
Milton, Ontario, 1999-

Virginia Wilson Toccalino and her husband, Tony Toccalino, working as a wife and husband team, have created beautiful glass objects for collectors. These include paperweights, orbs, eggs, unique ornaments, bells, and many other types of blown pieces. She received awards and scholarships to study with Venetian glass masters in the creation of murrini, complex cane, and filigrana techniques.

Virginia was the resident glassblower at the Ontario Renaissance Festival for nine years doing glassblowing demonstrations while Tony gave an informative commentary raising awareness of the wonders of glassblowing. During this time they built their own glass blowing facility in 1999.

In 2006 she began promoting her glass business with her name, Virginia Wilson Toccalino, using the logo VWT.
Virginia and Tony started making bells in 2001. All bells are made selecting the best and most uniform, consistent, patterned canes. Bell handles are made separately and carefully matched to their respective bell bodies. Virginia makes the clappers at the torch using matching colors, patterns, and canes. Recently, she made a signature cane, a rod of glass which has her initials in monogram form. Newer bells incorporate a slice of the rod with her initials.

The author thanks Virginia Wilson Toccalino for supplying the photographs and descriptions for these bells.

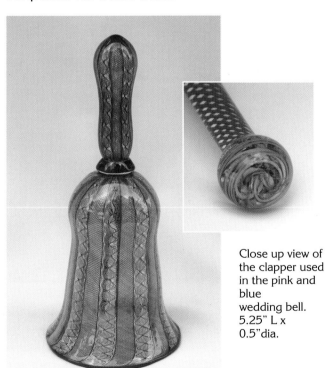

Close up view of the clapper used in the pink and blue wedding bell. 5.25" L x 0.5"dia.

A pink and blue magnum filigree wedding bell with blown handle. The stem of the clapper is made from the pink latticino cane matching the body of the bell and the ball is made from a pink and blue zanfirico cane used in the body. 5.5"dia. x 11.5"h. $800-900.

A peach and aqua magnum filigree wedding bell with blown handle. The stem of the clapper is made from the peach latticino cane matching the body of the bell and the ball is made from a peach and aqua zanfirico cane used in the body. 5.75"dia. x 12.25"h. $800-900.

A purple and green magnum filigree wedding bell with blown handle. The stem of the clapper is made from the purple latticino cane matching the body of the bell and the ball clapper is made from the green zanfirico cane used in the body. 5.5"dia. x 11.4"h. $800-900.

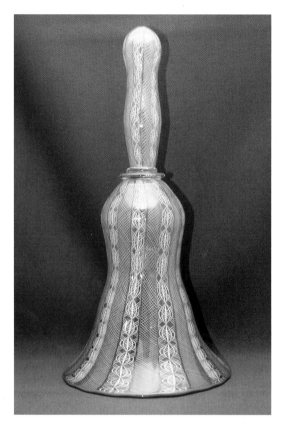

A close up view of the clapper belonging to the purple and green wedding bell. 5" L x 0.5"dia.

A mauve and lime magnum filigree wedding bell with blown handle. The stem of the clapper is made from the mauve latticino cane matching the body of the bell and the ball clapper is made from the lime zanfirico cane used in the body. 5.25"dia. x 11"h. $800-900.

A green and blue Damascus bell. Swirling colored canes create the pattern on this bell. It has a folded lip and a matching glass cane on the handle. The clapper stem is clear and the ball is blue. 4.5"dia. x 9.75"h. $200-240.

A green Damascus bell with stardust handle. Green swirling rods create the pattern on this bell. It has a folded lip and has stardust floating throughout the handle. The stem of the clapper is clear; the ball is green. $200-240.

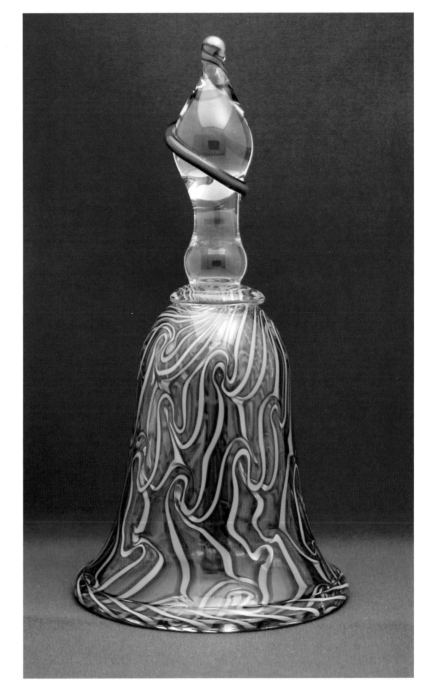

A pink Damascus bell with satin finish. Swirling colored canes create the pattern on this bell. It has a folded lip and matching glass cane on the handle. This bell has been lightly etched to achieve the satin finish. The clapper stem is clear; the ball is a pink and white swirl. 4.25"dia. x 8.25"h. $200-240.

Swirling colored canes create the pattern on this pink Damascus bell. It has a folded lip and matching glass cane on the handle. The clapper stem is clear, the ball is pink with a white swirl. 4"dia. x 8"h. $200-240.

Swirling colored canes create the pattern on this white Damascus bell. It has a folded lip and matching glass cane on the handle. The clapper stem is clear with a white ball. 4.1"dia. x 7.9"h. $200-240.

Swirling colored canes create the pattern on this yellow Damascus bell. It has a folded lip and matching glass cane on the handle. The clapper stem is clear with a yellow ball. 3.6"dia. x 8"h. $200-240.

Swirling colored canes create the pattern on this cobalt blue Damascus bell. It has a folded lip and matching glass cane on the handle. The clapper stem is clear with a cobalt ball. 4.4"dia. x 8.5"h. $200-240.

A satin swirl bell with air twist handle. Gently swirling brown canes and a folded lip decorate the body of this bell. The stem of the clapper is clear with a cobalt ball. 4.4"dia. x 9.25"h. $200-240.

This filigree bell displays zanfirico canes alternating with ribbon canes. The handle is made from a matching ribbon ring. The clapper stem is yellow zanfirico rod with a purple and yellow ball. 3.5"dia. x 5.5"h. $325-375.

This Christmas filigree Bell displays zanfirico canes alternating with ribbon canes. The handle is made from a matching zanfirico ring. The clapper is a white latticino rod with a matching ribbon glass ball. 3.1"dia. x 5.9"h. $325-375.

A close-up view of the 3.75" long black filigree clapper.

This black filigree bell with a flat handle displays zanfirico canes alternating with multi colored ribbon canes. The handle has a matching ribbon cane swirling gently down and around it. The clapper is a latticino stem with a ribbon ball. 3.1"dia. x 5.25"h. $325-375.

A pink filigree bell with a flat handle. This bell combines pink zanfirico canes with purple and blue ribbon canes. The handle has a complementary blue ribbon cane decorating it. The clapper stem is the pink zanfirico cane with a purple and blue ball. 3.1"dia. x 6.75"h. $325-375.

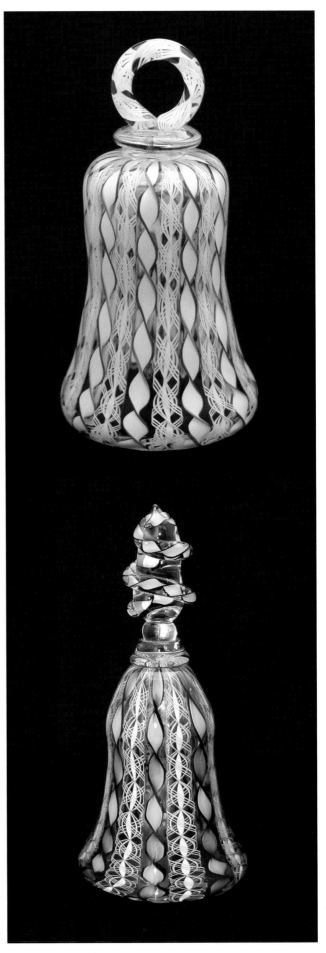

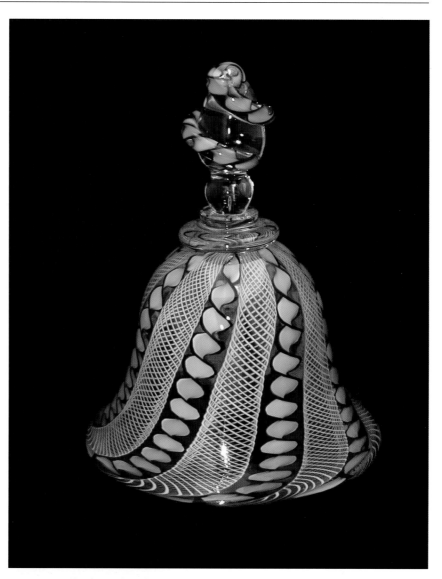

This is a ribbon cane bell combined with veil canes. Veil canes are made by forming tubes of color which are then filled with clear crystal. It has a matching ribbon cane on the handle. The stem of the clapper is a ruby veil cane with a ruby ball. 3.5"dia. x 8"h. $325-375.

A green and blue ribbon glass bell. This filigree bell displays ribbon canes alternating with latticino canes. The bell has a black lip wrap. The handle is made from a matching Zanfirico cane ring. The clapper is a latticino rod with a ribbon glass ball. 4"dia. x 5.4"h. $325-375.

Two ribbon glass bells with two different combinations of glass ribbon canes. One is green and blue ribbons with green latticino; the other is pink and purple ribbon canes with ruby veil canes. Unique handles and clapper stems are made with matching canes. Note the subtle symmetrical ruffles on these bells. Both have a contrasting black lip wrap. 3.75"dia. x 7.5"h. $325-375 each.

A view of the 3.75" long clapper for the purple and green ribbon glass bell.

A purple and green ribbon glass bell. This filigree bell displays ribbon canes alternating with latticino canes. The bell has a black lip wrap. The handle is made from a matching latticino cane ring. The clapper stem is the purple and green ribbon cane with a stardust ball. 3.75"dia. x 6.1"h. $325-375.

A red and brown filigree bell with vibrant brown zanfirico cane and red stripes. It has a matching red cane on the handle and the clapper stem is a brown zanfirico cane with a clear ball. 3.1"dia. x 7.4"h. $325-375.

A pink and brown filigree bell with unusual variegated brown ribbon cane and pink zanfirico cane combination. The bell has a black lip wrap. It has a matching ribbon cane ring handle. The clapper stem is a pink zanfirico cane and the ball is a swirling brown ribbon. 3.25"dia. x 5.2"h. $325-375.

This brown filigree bell has unusual brown zanfirico canes combined with amber ribbon canes with a hint of goldstone in them. The bell has a black lip wrap . The handle matches the body with the brown zanfirico cane. The clapper stem is a brown zanfirico cane with a swirling ribbon ball. 3.75"dia. x 5.5"h. $325-375.

This filigree bell has green zanfirico rods alternating with blue ribbon canes. The bell has a black lip wrap. It has a matching ribbon cane on the handle and the clapper stem is a green zanfirico rod with a blue swirling ball. 3.5"dia. x 8.2"h. $325-375.

A 4" long by 0.4" dia. white filigree clapper with a sterling silver attachment to the white filigree bell.

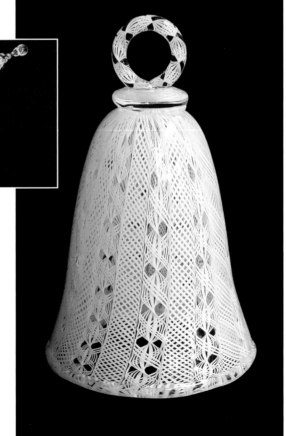

This white filigree Bell displays zanfirico canes alternating with latticino canes. The bell has a folded lip. The handle is made from a matching zanfirico ring. The white canes are a traditional favorite as all the lines have a sharp edge making this piece very distinctive. The clapper stem is a matching white latticino rod with a swirling white zanfirico ball. 3.75"dia. x 6.25"h. $325-375.

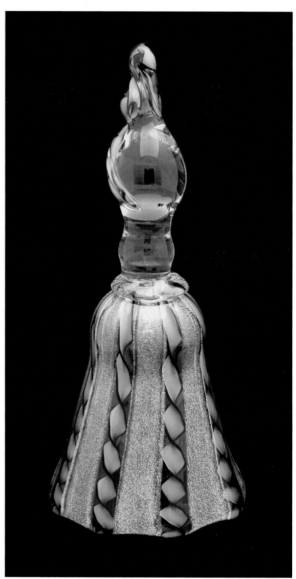

This stardust ribbon bell has a black lip wrap and a hint of a ruffle on the bottom of the body. The pointed handle has a matching ribbon cane gently swirling down two sides that matches the body of the bell. The clapper stem is a matching ribbon cane with a stardust ball. 3.25"dia. x 7.5"h. $525-575.

This is a multicolor ribbon stardust bell. It has a black lip wrap and a hint of a ruffle on the bottom of the body. The pointed handle has a matching ribbon cane gently swirling down two sides that matches the body of the bell. The clapper stem is a matching ribbon cane with a stardust ball. 4.1"dia. x 8.5"h. $725-775.

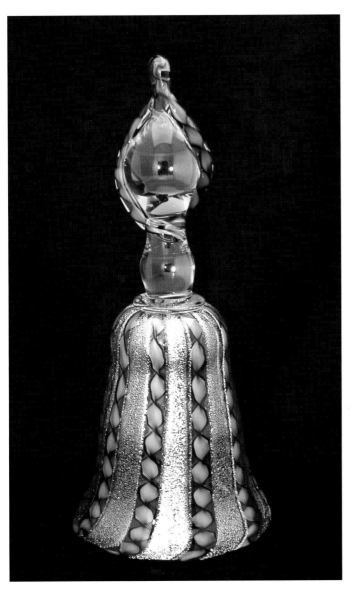

This violet stardust ribbon bell has a black lip wrap and a hint of a ruffle on the bottom of the body. The pointed handle has a matching ribbon cane gently swirling down two sides that matches the body of the bell. The clapper stem is a matching ribbon cane with a stardust ball. 3.5"dia. x 8"h. $425-475.

This blue and silver ruby filigree stardust bell has a natural ruffle on the bottom of the body. The pointed handle has a matching zanfirico cane gently swirling down two sides that matches the body of the bell. The clapper stem is a matching zanfirico cane with a stardust ball. $525-575.

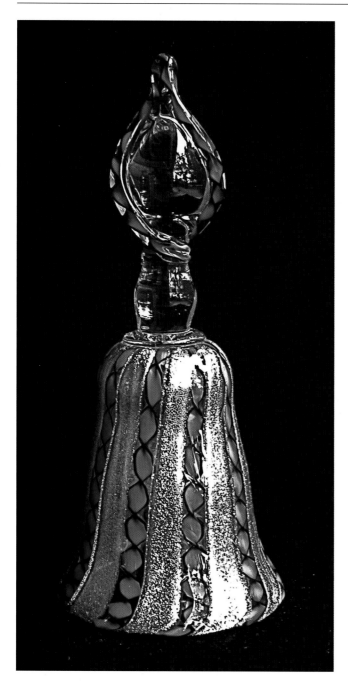

This orange filigree stardust bell has a hint of a ruffle on the bottom of the body. The pointed handle has a matching zanfirico cane gently swirling down two sides that matches the body of the bell. The clapper stem is a matching zanfirico cane with a stardust ball. 4.25"dia. x 9.75"h. $725-775.

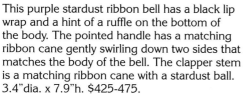

This purple stardust ribbon bell has a black lip wrap and a hint of a ruffle on the bottom of the body. The pointed handle has a matching ribbon cane gently swirling down two sides that matches the body of the bell. The clapper stem is a matching ribbon cane with a stardust ball. 3.4"dia. x 7.9"h. $425-475.

This unusual filigree stardust bell has two decorative crystal leaves applied to the top of the body which has a hint of a ruffle at the bottom . The pointed handle has a matching zanfirico cane gently swirling down two sides that matches the body of the bell. The clapper stem is a matching zanfirico cane with a stardust ball. 4.1"dia. x 10"h. $725-775.

This blue and green filigree stardust bell has a hint of a ruffle on the bottom of the body. The pointed handle has a matching ribbon rod gently swirling down two sides that matches the body of the bell. The clapper stem is a matching ribbon cane with a stardust ball. $425-475.

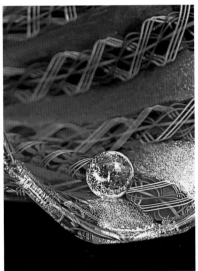

Close-up view of the cobalt blue and green filigree stardust bell clapper. Note the filigree stem of the clapper with the stardust ball to match the body of the bell. Signed Virginia Wilson Toccalino.

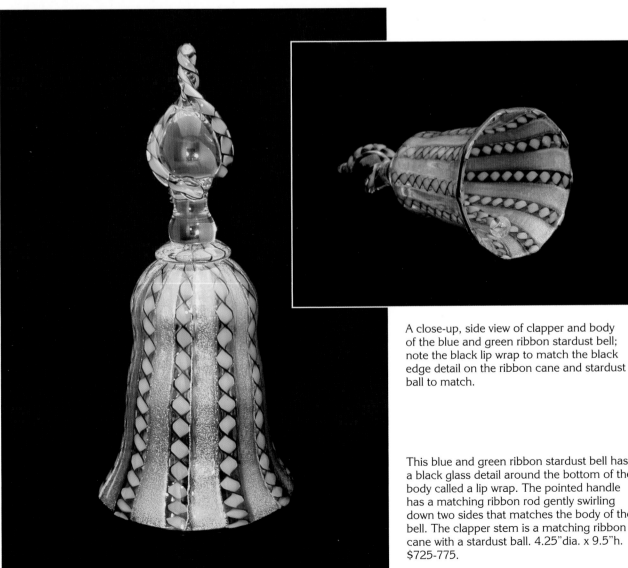

A close-up, side view of clapper and body of the blue and green ribbon stardust bell; note the black lip wrap to match the black edge detail on the ribbon cane and stardust ball to match.

This blue and green ribbon stardust bell has a black glass detail around the bottom of the body called a lip wrap. The pointed handle has a matching ribbon rod gently swirling down two sides that matches the body of the bell. The clapper stem is a matching ribbon cane with a stardust ball. 4.25"dia. x 9.5"h. $725-775.

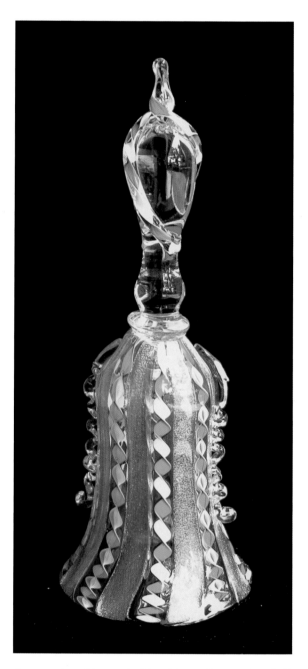

This pink and green ribbon stardust bell has a black lip wrap detail and a hint of a ruffle on the bottom of the body. The cane on the handle matches the body of the bell. The clapper stem is a matching ribbon cane with a stardust ball. 4.25"dia. x 9.1"h. $725-775.

A very unique blue and white ribbon silver stardust bell in that it has a clear pinched trail decoration running down two sides. It has a black lip wrap detail and a hint of a ruffle on the bottom of the body. A blue and white ribbon cane comes to a point at the top of an extended handle. The clapper stem is a matching ribbon cane with a stardust ball. 4"dia. x 10.4"h.

A white and silver stardust Christmas bell has a single crystal leaf decoration at the top of its ruffled body. A matching white zanfirico cane swirls gracefully down the handle. The clapper has a matching zanfirico cane stem with a stardust ball. 4.5"dia. x 9.6"h. $725-775.

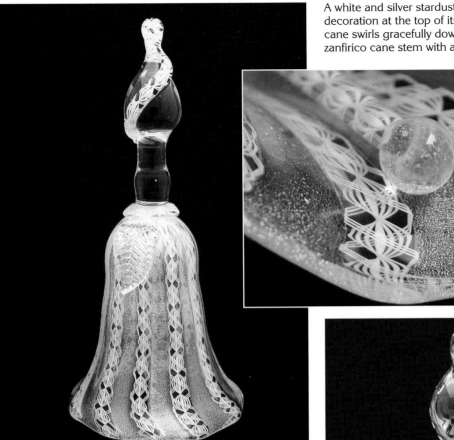

A close-up view of the clapper and bottom edge of the white and silver stardust Christmas bell. Note the perfectly executed white zanfirico canes and the contrasting brilliant shimmer of the silver stardust glass in the body of this bell and clapper.

This large purple ribbon stardust bell has a black glass detail around the bottom of the body called a lip wrap. The pointed handle has a matching ribbon rod gently swirling down two sides that matches the body of the bell. The clapper stem is a matching ribbon cane with a stardust ball. 4.1"dia. x 10.4"h. $725-775.

The pink and blue rods used in this bell are known as zanfirico complex canes. They are perfectly matched and executed in this spectacular stardust bell. The lovely pointed handle has a matching rod decorating it. The body of the bell has a black lip wrap detail at the bottom. The clapper has a matching zanfirico cane stem with a stardust ball. 4.6"dia. x 9.75"h. $725-775.

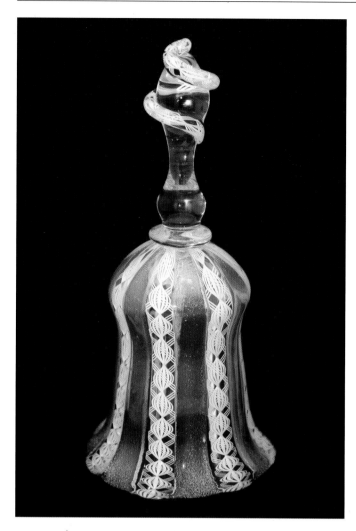

This white filigree stardust bell has a matching white zanfirico cane swirling gracefully around the long handle. The clapper has a matching zanfirico cane stem with a stardust ball. There is a black lip wrap detail and a hint of a ruffle on the bottom of the bell. 3.75"dia. x 8.5"h. $725-775.

A red and white ribbon silver stardust Christmas bell. The pointed handle has a matching ribbon rod gently swirling down two sides that matches the body. The clapper stem is a matching ribbon cane with a stardust ball. This bell is a good example of the consistent twist and placement of cane that exhibits the undeviating pattern that is indicative of bells made by Virginia Wilson Toccalino and Tony Toccalino. 3.5"dia. x 7.1"h. $425-475.

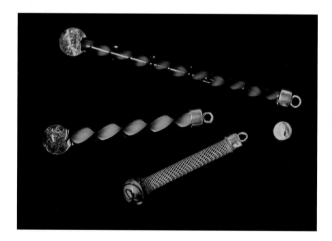

All the clappers used in the Virginia Wilson Toccalino bells have clappers with stems and balls that match the decoration on the body of the respective bell pattern. The picture shows bell clappers ready to be installed in their respective bells bodies. The caps are sterling silver and were custom made specifically to fit the rods.

A signature cane is a glass rod that has been hand built with the makers initials running up the length of the rod. A slice of the rod displaying the initials is snipped off and placed somewhere on the piece being made and used to identify the maker. All future bells created by Virginia Wilson Toccalino will have a signature murrini somewhere on the bell. Bells without signature murrini are signed with an engraved signature, identifying earlier work.

The next four photos of Galactic Art Glass Studio bells are from the collection of Sally and Rob Roy.

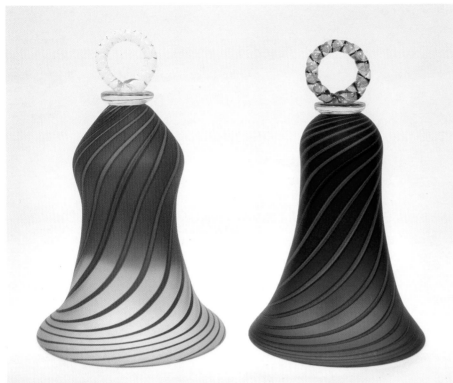

A rose glass bell with a gold swirl on the left and a blue glass bell with a gold swirl on the right. 4.25"dia. x 6.75"h. and 4"dia. x 6.5"h. $100-150 each. Left bell is unsigned. The right bell is signed "V. Wilson Toccalino 02". *Courtesy of Sally and Rob Roy.*

This photo shows the horizontal bridge holding a clapper. *Courtesy of Sally and Rob Roy.*

A Latticino pattern glass bell with an elaborate handle. 4.6"dia. x 9.4"h. Signed "V. Wilson Toccalino" $450-500. *Courtesy of Sally and Rob Roy.*

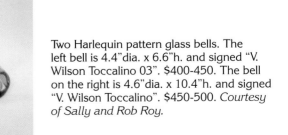

Two Harlequin pattern glass bells. The left bell is 4.4"dia. x 6.6"h. and signed "V. Wilson Toccalino 03". $400-450. The bell on the right is 4.6"dia. x 10.4"h. and signed "V. Wilson Toccalino". $450-500. *Courtesy of Sally and Rob Roy.*

Snookum Art Glass, Inc.
Calgary, Alberta, 1978-1982

Robert Held Art Glass
Vancouver, British Columbia, 1982-

Robert Held started glass blowing and teaching at Sheridan College, Ontario, in 1969. In 1978 he left the teaching world and started Snookum Art Glass, Inc. Here he produces many glass sculptures with occasional bells.

Three Robert Held glass bells with the center bell having pink swirls with the other two with blue swirls. Left to right: 2.6"dia. x 8.75"h., 3.5"dia. x 10.4"h., and 3.5"dia. x 8.5"h. $50-60 each. *Courtesy of Sally and Rob Roy.*

Three Robert Held glass bells. The left bell is clear glass with parallel blue ribbons and a twisted clear glass handle. 2.75"dia. x 8.9"h. The middle bell has chevron stripes and a twisted colorless handle. 3"dia. x 8"h. The bell on the right is clear colorless glass with striping of various shades of blue and a fluted handle. 2.9"dia. x 6.9"h. $50-60 each. *Courtesy of Sally and Rob Roy.*

Four Robert held glass bells. Left to right: the two left bells are dark green with colorless handles. 2.5"dia. x 7.75"h. and 3.4"dia. x 9"h.; the third bell from the left is clear pale blue. 2.75"dia. x 7.5"h.; the bell on the right is dark blue with a clear colorless rim and a colorless handle with twisted blue ribbons and a flat round top. 3.5"dia. x 8.75"h. $50-70 each. *Courtesy of Sally and Rob Roy.*

Rossi Glass, Inc.
Niagara Falls, Ontario, 1996-

Rossi Glass is known for a variety of blown glass articles particularly in cranberry glass. In 1997 the company started making table lamps. The company has a team of glassmakers from Europe and Canada. A variety of bells are known.

The firm was established by Angelo Rossi, but he left in 2001 and taught glassmaking at several universities in the United States. In 1904 he returned to Canada and established the Artistic Glass Blowing Studio in Niagara Falls. The author is not aware of any glass bells made in that studio.

A Rossi Glass gold cranberry glass bell with vertical ribbing and a colorless handle with a molded "R" on top. 4.5"dia. x 7"h. $40-50.

A Rossi Glass ribbed gold metallic glass bell with flared rim. "R" is on top of the handle. 3.75"dia. x 5.5"h. $60-70. *Courtesy of Mary and Ken Moyer.*

A Rossi milk glass bell with blue and rust colored spots and a clear colorless handle. 4"dia. x 6.25"h. $60-70. *Courtesy of Mary and Ken Moyer.*

A Rossi cranberry glass bell with a clear colorless twisted handle. 3.5"dia. x 7.5"h. $60-70. *Courtesy of Mary and Ken Moyer.*

European Bells

Austria

Several factories in Austria have produced glass bells.

Palda Glas
Haida, Novi Bor, 1888-1938

Palda Glas is usually associated with Bohemia, but the bell shown has a label stating "Palda Glas, Made in Austria, Ollern"

An Austrian Karl Palda clear green glass bell with artistic decoration, ruffled rim, and golden handle. c.1930s. 3.4"dia. x 5.25"h. $100-125.

Austrian bells of unknown manufacture

An Austrian clear glass bell with an engraved vintage pattern and 4 knop handle. c.1980. 4.5"dia. x 8.25"h. $35-40.

An Austrian clear glass bell with gold ruffled rim and with a crystal and golden covered owl handle. c.1987. 2.25"dia. x 5.1"h. $30-35.

Belgium

Val St. Lambert
Liège, 1825-

During the period 1939-1977 Val St. Lambert produced many bells.

A Val St. Lambert clear glass bell with four rows of a triangular pattern. PASCO label. 2.75"dia. x 5.75"h. $30-35.

A blue cut to clear Val St. Lambert glass bell with a diamond and cross-cut diamond pattern. There is a VSL engraved near the base of the handle. 3.8"dia. x 7.5"h. $125-150.

A Belgian clear glass bell with etched flowers and spiral air twist handle. c.1976. 5.25"dia. x 10"h. $40-50.

A Val St. Lambert clear green glass bell with a cross-cut diamond pattern and clear colorless hexagonal tapered cut handle, 2.75"dia. x 4.75"h. $20-30.

A Val St. Lambert clear glass bell with a radial and cross-cut diamond pattern. 2.6"dia. x 5.1"h. $30-35.

Bohemia

Before World War 1 many factories produced glass articles in Austria, Czechoslovakia, Germany, and Poland in an area known as Bohemia.

Two older bells are known from the earlier Bohemian period.

A Bohemian ruby glass bell with 13 facetted sides and elaborate bronze handle. c.1850. 2.9"dia. x 5.5"h. $575-625.

A Bohemian 4 layer cut glass bell in red over mustard, over white, cut to clear glass in oval panels. Silver coated bronze dolphin handle. c.1850. $400-500.

Czechoslovakia
1918-1993

Czech Republic
1993-

After World War 1 Czechoslovakia was formed. Some bells are known from that period. In 1993 The Czech Republic and Slovakia were formed from what was formerly Czechoslovakia.

Some Czech Republic bells are from unknown manufacturers.

A Czech Republic light amber flashed glass bell with a winter scene. 3"dia. x 5.5"h. $30-40.

A Czech Republic clear cranberry glass bell with clear colorless handle. c.1975. 3.4"dia. x 6"h. $20-30.

A Czech Republic multicolor satin glass bell with a long handle. c.1978. 3.1"dia. x 9.25"h. $25-35.

A Czech Republic clear glass bell with a facetted knob handle and a clear knop with gilt fish decoration. The green diamond pattern base has a serrated rim. The top of the handle has many facets. 3.5"dia. x 4.6"h. $40-50.

Below:
A Czech Republic frosted and clear glass bell with gold decoration and vintage pattern. 3.25"dia. x 6"h. $30-35.

A Czech Republic cranberry glass bell with molded diamond pattern and clear colorless loop handle. 3.9"dia. x 4.75"h. $25-30.

A Czech Republic purple glass bell with a cut to clear design. 3"dia. x 5.5"h. $45-55. *Courtesy of Mary and Ken Moyer.*

A Czech Republic clear glass bell with engraved scroll and grapes with a hexagonal handle. 2.9"dia. x 4.6"h. $25-35.

A Czech Republic blue glass bell with floral decoration and clear glass handle with 3 gold rings. 2.6"dia. x 5.9"h. $25-35.

A Czech Republic clear blue glass bell with decorated gold rim and clear colorless two part twisted handle with one knop. 2.5"dia. x 6.25"h. $30-40.

Antonin Rückl
1992-1998

Rückl Crystal A/S
Nižbor, 1998-

The current company is connected to a 300-year-long tradition of glass-making. Glass bells are known from recent years.

A Czech Republic clear red glass bell with gold grape decoration and clear colorless twisted glass handle made by Rukl & Sons for Ofnah. 3.25"dia. x 6.75"h. $30-40.

Denmark

Holmegaard Glassworks A/S
Fensmarck, 1977-

Holmegaard Glassworks celebrated its 175 jubilee in 2000.
Today it is part of Royal Scandinavia A/S in Frederiksberg.
Some clear glass bells are known in various colors.

A Holmegaard blue glass bell with a wood clapper. This bell can also
be found in other colors. 3.5"dia. x 5"h. $30-35.

France

Bells from several French companies are known.

Cristalleries Royales de Champagne
Bayel, 1666-

Bayel has produced many glass bells. Some clear crystal bells with frosted handles of animals and historic figures can be found.

A Bayel clear glass bell with a 25th anniversary decoration. c.1973. 3"dia. x 6"h. $20-25.

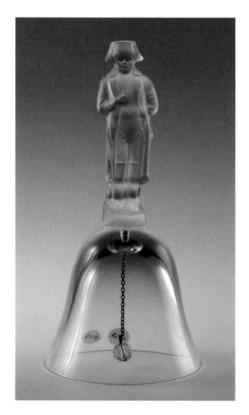

A Bayel clear glass bell with a frosted glass Napoleon handle. 3.25"dia. x 6.25"h. $30-40.

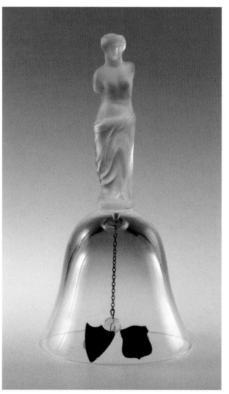

A Bayel clear glass bell with a frosted glass Venus de Milo handle. c.1979. 3.4"dia. x 6.9"h. $30-40.

A Bayel clear glass bell with an amber glass rim. 3.4"dia. x 4.6"h. $25-30.

Cristallerie Daum
Nancy, 1962-

Glass bells produced by Daum usually are signed "Daum, France" with a small engraved Cross of Lorraine.

Flint glass bells. Some square shaped glass bells with assorted metal handles and clappers are known from the 19th century. The current consensus is that most of the glass was made in France and the handles made in the German part of Europe.

An amber flint glass bell with a bronze devil as the handle and a pitchfork as the clapper. 1.9"sq. x 4"h. $1,200-1,500. *Courtesy of Sally and Rob Roy.*

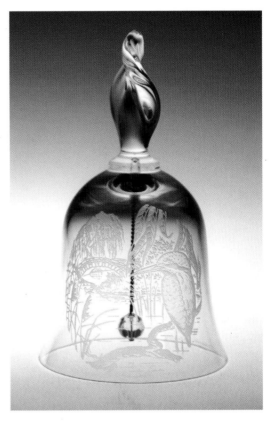

A Daum clear glass bell with an etched kingfisher scene. Signed Daum, France. 3.25"dia. x 5.75"h. $75-85.

A pair of blue flint glass bells. The bell on the left has a bronze anchor handle with a miniature sailboat. On the sailboat is an R11 over 19. Two persons are putting up the sail . 1.9"sq. x 4.5"h. The bell on the right has a bronze handle coat of arms of the United Kingdom of Great Britain and Northern Ireland with the motto "Dieu et mon droit" (God and my right). The shield is supported by an English Lion on the left and the Unicorn of Scotland on the right. The coat of arms also features the motto of the Order of the Garter: "Honi soit qui mal y pense" (Evil to him who evil thinks) on a representation of the Garter behind the shield. 1.9"sq. x 4"h. $600-700 each. *Courtesy of Sally and Rob Roy.*

A flint blue glass bell with a bull handle on a base with turquoise enamel and a matador's sword clapper with the sword wrapped in fine red silk thread. 1.9"sq. x 3.1"h. $1,500-2,000. *Courtesy of Sally and Rob Roy.*

Some older opaline glass bells are from an unknown manufacturer.

Four French translucent opaline glass bells. Left to right: white glass bell with painted flower and gold decoration. 2.75"dia. x 4.25"h.; white glass with gilded leaves and violet flower decoration, 2.75"dia. x 4.1"h.; white glass with gilded flowers and leaves, 2.6"dia. x 4"h.; pink glass with gilded floral decoration, 2.9"dia. x 4.1"h. $55-65 each.

Some bells are made in France, but the manufacturer is currently unknown.

A ruby 10 panel glass bell with an ivory carved Napoleon handle. 2.9"dia. x 6"h. $750-900. *Courtesy of Sally and Rob Roy.*

A blue cut to clear 8 panel glass bell with a bronze handle. 3.25"dia. x 4.75"h. $900-1,000. *Courtesy of Sally and Rob Roy.*

**West Germany
1949-1990**

House of Goebel

Many items have been produced over the years under the name of House of Goebel. Among them are some bells.

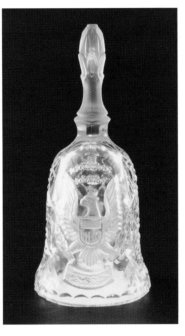

A House of Goebel blue and clear pressed glass bell with a hobstar, fan, and stripes pattern. 2.75"dia. x 5.5"h. $20-25.

A Goebel clear pressed three mold glass bell with eagle and 13 stars and a frosted glass handle. 3.5"dia. x 8"h. $25-30.

A Goebel clear glass bell with a six panel shoulder and three knop handle. Signed "Goebel 1982". 2.9"dia. x 6.1"h. $40-50.

Graf Schaffgottsch'sche Josephinenhutte

Glass objects made under the name Josephinenhutte are known from Bohemia from the nineteenth and early twentieth century, but more recent glass, including bells, has been sold under the name Josair.

A West German Josair clear 8 facets glass bell, with engraved flowers on one facet, and hexagonal handle. c.1976. 3"dia. x 5.4"h. $50-55.

Other West German bells are of unknown manufacturer.

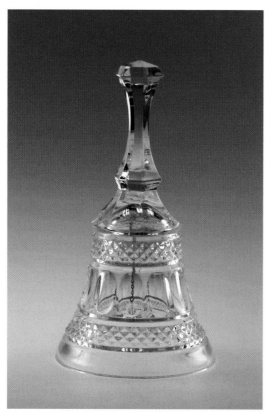

A West German clear pressed glass bell with a cross-cut diamonds and punties pattern. 3.4"dia. x 6.4"h. $20-25.

A West German pale olive green clear glass bell with a twisted handle. 2.1"dia. x 5.75"h. $25-30.

A West German clear glass bell with floral engraving made for Tiffany. 2.5"dia. x 4.5"h. $30-35.

A West German very dark red glass bell with a clear colorless handle. 2.9"dia. x 4.9"h. $40-50.

Alfred Taub, Vohenstrauss, GmbH

Some clear glass bells with floral decoration can
be found with the Alfred Taub label.

A West German Alfred Taub clear glass bell with
painted flowers. 2.75"dia. x 5"h. $30-35.

A West German Alfred Taub flashed red glass bell
with engraved scenes. 2.75"dia. x 5"h. $30-35.

East Germany

An East German bell is from an unknown manufacturer.

An East German clear glass bell with etched grapes and twisted handle. 3.1"dia. x 7"h. $30-40.

Dresden Crystal

Lausitzer Glashuette, AG
Döbern, 2005-

In 1969 several state owned companies merged to become Lausitzer Glas. A few glass bells were produced. Dresden Crystal is now a part of Lausitzer Glashuette, AG.

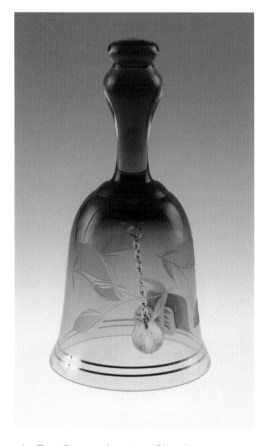

An East German Lausitzer Glas clear green glass bell with engraved heart shaped leaves and two gold stripes. 2.5"dia. x 5.1"h.

Two East German Lausitzer Glas bells in purple cut to clear glass with applied floral and gold decoration. 3.75"dia. x 9.25"h. and 3"dia. x 6.5"h. $80-100 each.

Hungary

Several Hungarian bells are known, but their manufacturer is presently unknown to the author.

A pair of Hungarian clear glass bells with painted flowers made for the Crystal Clear Importing Co. 3.6"dia. x 7.25"h. $25-30 each.

Ireland

Cavan Crystal Designs Ltd.
Cavan, 1969-

Cavan Crystal has produced several kinds of crystal items, including bells.

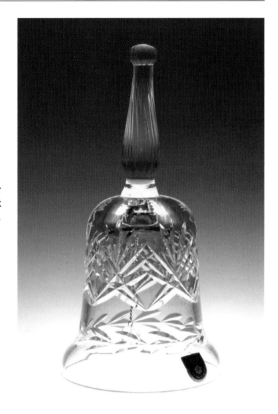

A Cavan Crystal clear glass bell. 3.9"dia. x 7.75"h. $25-30.

A Failte clear glass bell with a clear and red glass air twist handle. 5.6"dia. x 7.25"h. $25-30.

Failte Crystal
Dublin, 1971-

Failte Crystal is known for items with intaglio engraving. The bell shown is known with a Failte label.

Galway Irish Crystal Ltd.
Merlin Park, Galway, 1993-

Several glass bells are known from the company. Galway Irish Crystal was acquired by Belleek Pottery Ltd. in 1993.

A Galway Crystal clear glass bell with a diamond and punty pattern and a hexagonal handle. 3.25"dia. x 6.9"h. $25-30.

A Galway Crystal bell with a Claddagh Ring etch. 2"dia. x 5.1"h. $20-30.

Israel

Several producers of glass bells are known in Israel.

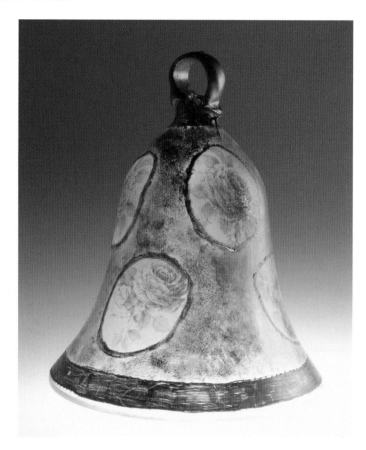

Jenny Kravits
Notivot, Israel

Jenny Kravits has produced several bells painted on a clear glass blank.

An Israel clear glass bell with painted roses and gold decoration by Jenny Kravits. 8.5"dia. x 10.75"h. $50-60.

Some bells can be found from an unknown manufacturer.

A pair of Israel clear blown glass bells. Left to right: blue bell, 4.25"dia. x 6"h.; green bell, 3.25"dia. x 4.5"h. $25-30 each. *Courtesy of Mary and Ken Moyer.*

Italy

Glass bells have been made in various parts of Italy,
but primarily on the island of Murano.

An Italian pink glass bell with applied
white glass flower on an amber stem
and amber twisted round handle.
3.6"dia. x 4.75"h. $50-60.

An Italian olive green clear glass bell with an engraved lily of the valley design. A "G" is on the
top of the handle. c.1970. 3.5"dia. x 6"h. $45-55.

An Italian clear red glass bell with an engraved floral design. 2.75"dia. x 4.75"h. $40-50.

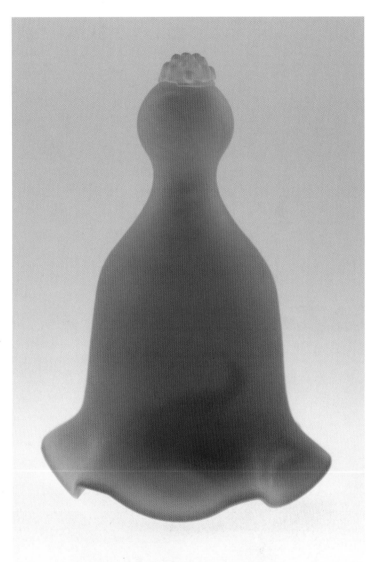

An Italian frosted green glass bell with applied flowers and colorless loop handle. 4.5"dia. x 5.6"h. $60-75.

An Italian Burmese glass bell with a mottled top of handle. 3.1"dia. x 4.5"h. $40-45.

An Italian clear red glass bell with applied flowers and colorless round handle. 3.75"dia. x 6.5"h. $25-30.

An Italian variegated violet glass bell with a ruffled rim and loop handle. 4.25"dia. x 6"h. $40-50.

An Arte Italica clear glass bell with a silver overlay design. 3.5"dia. x 6"h. $30-40.

An Italian multi-colored clear glass bell with a hexagonal cut glass handle with a red, white, & blue flower on the round knop. 4.5"dia. x 5.75"h. $40-50.

A pair of Toscany frosted glass bells with applied floral decoration. 3.5"dia. x 6.5"h. $30-40 each

Six Murano clown glass bells. Front left to right: dark blue, red, light blue, each 4"dia. x 6"h.; back row left to right: dark red, 4"dia. x 7"h., green, 4.25"dia. x 7.25"h, orange, 3.75"dia. x 7"h. $75-100 each. *Courtesy of Mary and Ken Moyer.*

An Italian "Rosa di Palma" clear pressed glass bell with a diamond and vesica pattern. 2.1"dia. x 4.5"h. $20-25.

A Crisa clear glass bell with floral decoration. 2.5"dia. x 4.5"h. $25-30.

A Crisa multi-facetted clear glass bell with an oblong loop handle. 3.1"dia. x 6.75"h. $30-40.

An Italian clear glass bell with a honeycomb pattern and zipper cut handle edges and rim. 3"dia. x 6.25"h. $40-60.

A Crisa clear swirled glass bell with an air twist loop handle. 3.75"dia. x 5.5"h. $30-40.

A Murano Nailsea type orange glass bell. 3.5"dia. x 4.5"h. $55-65. *Courtesy of Mary and Ken Moyer.*

Three Murano clown handle glass bells. Left to right: blue, 4"dia. x 6.5"h.; dark red, 3.5"dia. x 6.5"h.; and green, 4.5"dia. x 7"h. $75-100 each. *Courtesy of Mary and Ken Moyer.*

Seven Murano Millefiore clown bells. 3.5"dia. x 6.5"h. $60-75 each. *Courtesy of Mary and Ken Moyer.*

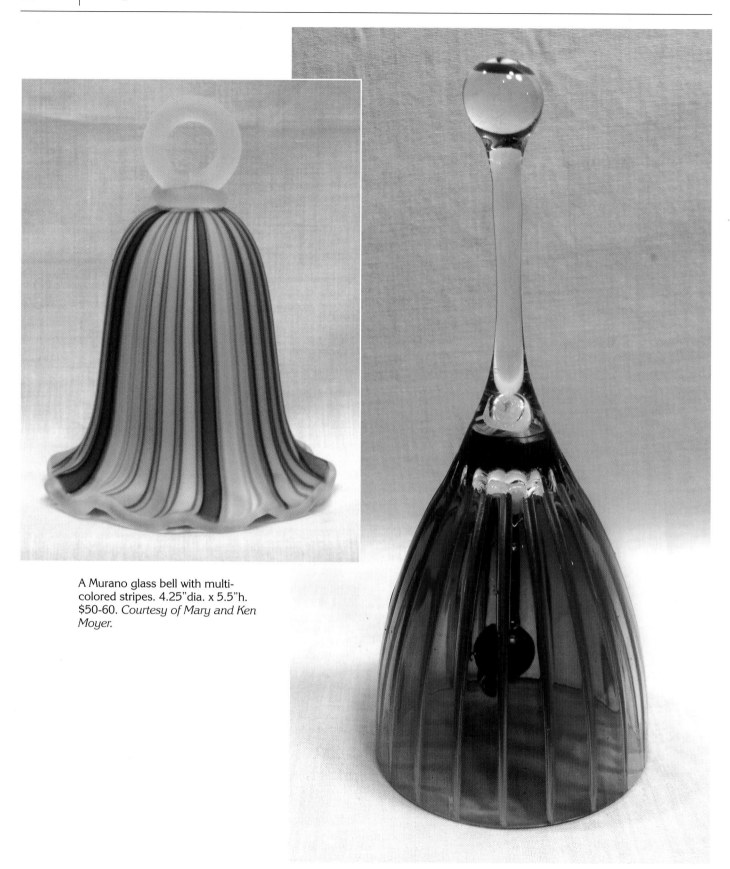

A Murano glass bell with multi-colored stripes. 4.25"dia. x 5.5"h. $50-60. *Courtesy of Mary and Ken Moyer.*

A Murano multi-colored stripes glass bell with a clear colorless handle. 2.25"dia. x 5.25"h. $45-55. *Courtesy of Mary and Ken Moyer.*

A red clear glass bell with a diamond pattern and a clear colorless triangular shape handle. 4.5"dia. x 6.5"h. $45-55. *Courtesy of Mary and Ken Moyer.*

A Murano hand painted multi-colored glass bell. 2.25"dia. x 4.75"h. $30-40. *Courtesy of Mary and Ken Moyer.*

A Murano cranberry glass bell with a colorless angel handle. 3.5"dia. x 7.5"h. $50-60.

A Murano blue and white glass bell with a colorless glass angel handle. 3.5"dia. x 9"h. $60-70.

Norway

Hadeland Glassverk A/S
Jevnaker, Oppland, 1762-

The original glassworks was founded in 1762. Today it is a glass division of Royal Scandinavia. A few recent glass bells are known.

A Hadeland clear glass bell. 2.4"dia. x 5.4"h. $30-35

Poland

Krosno, S. A.
Krosno, 1923

Krosno manufactures many glass products. A few bells are known.

A Krosno crystal bell in very light clear blue glass with a cut floral pattern and a three part handle. 2.5"dia. x 4.5"h. $25-35.

A Polish clear amber glass bell with floral engraving. c.1980. 2.25"dia. x 4.5"h. $25-30

Portugal

Atlantis, S. A.
Alcobaça, 1997-

The company, as a division of Salton, Inc., has produced several bells.

An Atlantis clear glass bell with a fluted pattern. Signed "Atlantis". 2.75"dia. x 5.75"h. $30-40.

A Portuguese bell from an unknown manufacturer.

A clear glass bell from Portugal with an engraved floral decoration and twisted tapered handle. 3.5"dia. x 6.5"h. $20-25.

Romania

Several bells have a sticker showing that they were made in Romania, but the manufacturer is unknown at this time.

A Romanian clear glass bell with engraved flowers. 3.75"dia. x 8.25"h. $35-45.

A Romanian leaded stain glass bell with a twisted spiral handle. 3.5"dia. x 7"h. $75-80.

Serbia

A Serbian bell from Rogaska Glassverk is known.

A Serbian Rogaska Glassverk clear glass bell with a diamond pattern and etched flowers. 2.1"dia. x 2.75"h. $25-30.

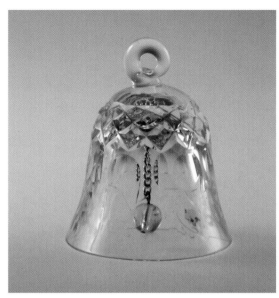

Slovakia

Bells from an unknown manufacturer are known.

A Slovakian clear green glass bell with a vertical vine cutting. 2.6"dia. x 6.25"h. $30-40.

A Slovakian clear glass bell with a cut floral pattern. 3"dia. x 6.75"h. $25-30.

Slovenia

Bells from an unknown manufacturer have been produced.

A Slovenian clear multi-faceted glass bell with cut stars made for Mikasa. 2.6"dia. x 3.5"h. $25-30.

Spain

Vidrios de Arte Gordiola, S.L.
Algaida, Balearic Islands (Mallorca), 1719-

Glass articles have been produced on the island of Mallorca for several centuries. During the 1964-1965 New York World's Fair several bells made by Vidrios Gordiola appeared for sale in the Spanish Pavilion.

A blue Vidrios Gordiola threaded glass bell. c.1964. 3.25"dia. x 7.25"h. $250-350.

Sweden

Ekenas Glasbruk
Ekenas, 1917-1976

Ekenas was founded by some glass workers from Orrefors. The company produced a wide range of glass products, but very few bells.

A Swedish Ekenas heavy crystal bell with an air twist handle. 4.6"dia. x 7.75"h. $70-80.

Mantorp Glasbruk AB
Mantorp, 1968-

Mantorp has produced a variety of glass products including some bells.

A Mantorp clear green glass bell. 1.6"dia. x 3.5"h. $20-30.

Orrefors Glasbruk
Orrefors, 1898-

Orrefors has produced many glass products including a few bells.

A pair of Orrefors clear glass bells. The left bell has painted flowers in a "Maja" pattern with a silver handle. Signed EEAL for Eva English. 3"dia. x 4.25"h. The bell on the right is plain with the silver handle and clapper typical of many Orrefors bells. 2.5"dia. x 3.6"h. $40-45 each.

A glass bell from Sweden is from an unknown manufacturer.

A clear glass bell with an air twist handle. It has a "Made in Sweden" label. 4.4"dia. x 8.75"h. $60-75.

Switzerland

Very few Swiss glass bells are known to the author.

A Swiss clear cobalt glass bell with floral and gold overlay. 2.25"dia. x 4.1"h. $30-35.

United Kingdom

Burns Crystal Company
Mauchline, Ayrshire, Scotland, 1987-

Burns Crystal specializes in engraved and cut crystal products. A limited quantity of bells has been produced.

A Burns Crystal clear glass bell with an etched deer and "Balmaha, Loch Lomond" with an air twist handle. 2.6"dia. x 5.1"h. $45-50.

Caithness Glass, Ltd.
Perth, Scotland

1961 - Caithness Glass was founded in Wick, Scotland.
1988 – Caithness Glass acquires Wedgwood Crystal
1989-1992 - Caithness Crystal, King's Lynn,
1996 - Royal Doulton acquired Caithness Glass.
2001 - Royal Worcester and Spode Limited acquired Caithness Glass.
2004 – Royal Worchester sold Caithness to Edinburgh Crystal.
2006 – Dartington Crystal acquired Caithness Glass.

Caithness Glass has produced bells in clear and colored engraved glass.

A Caithness Glass clear crystal bell with an etched mistletoe. 2"dia. x 3.5"h. $30-35.

A pair of Caithness Glass crystal bells. The left blue glass bell is 2.9"dia. x 5.9"h. The yellow glass bell is 3.75"dia. x 6.25"h. $45-50 each.

Dartington Glass
Torrington, Devon, 1966-1987

Dartington Crystal, Ltd.
Linden Close, Torrington, Devon, 1987-

The founding company was started by Dartington Hall Trust, a development agency. They employed a Swedish glass-maker, Eskil Vilhemson, as managing director. He trained a team of Swedish glassblowers to start company operations. For twenty years the chief designer was Frank Thrower.
In 2004 the company and Royal Brierley Crystal were acquired by Enesco Limited, but in 2006 Enesco sold the company and Royal Brierley to the Dartington Crystal management group.
Many kinds of glass items have been produced including some bells. Most of the bells were designed by Frank Thrower and made between 1980 and 1983 in clear glass.

Dartington clear glass bell with etched Neptune and with "RGC" on the base of the handle. 3.1"dia. x 4.6"h. $45-50.

A Dartington clear glass bell. 3.5"dia. x 6.1"h. $40-45.

A James Deakin colorless crystal bell with a silver shoulder and handle hallmarked "Chester 1901" 3.5"dia. x 6.25"h. $200-225. *Courtesy of Sally and Rob Roy.*

James Deakin
Sheffield, 1865-1886

James Deakin & Sons
1886-1897

James Deakin & Sons, Ltd.
1897-1936

The firm was primarily a silver manufacturing company. A glass bell is known with silver handle and shoulder.

The Edinburgh and Leith Flint Glass Company
Edinburgh, Scotland, 1867-1955

The Edinburgh Crystal Glass Company
Edinburgh, Scotland, 1955-1969
Penicuik, Scotland, 1969-

The Edinburgh Crystal Glass Company has a long history of producing glass articles since its founding in 1867.

In 1921 Thomas Webb and Sons Ltd. acquired Edinburgh Crystal but it continued to operate under its own name.

In 1964 Crown House Ltd. acquired the Edinburgh Crystal Glass Company and Thomas Webb and Sons. In 1969 Edinburgh Crystal moved to Penicuik

In 1971 both firms were merged with Dema Glass, a Crown House subsidiary.

In 1987 Edinburgh Crystal and Thomas Webb were incorporated into the Coloroll Group.

In 1990 Caledonia Investments led a buyout of the Edinburgh Crystal Glass Company and the Thomas Webb and Sons brand.

Glass bells have been produced by the firm since the 1980s.

An Edinburgh Crystal clear glass bell with engraved floral pattern and a square tapered handle with cut corners. 3.6"dia. x 7.9"h. $140-150.

An Edinburgh Crystal clear glass bell with a cross-cut diamond and fan pattern and a large bubble in the handle. 4"dia. x 7.75"h. $50-60.

Gleneagles of Edinburgh, Ltd.
Aberdeen, Scotland, 1980s-1998

Gleneagles Crystal Company, Ltd.
1998-2002

Gleneagles Crystal produced hand cut glass articles. A few bells are known. Some under the Preciosa name were made in the Czech Republic.

A Gleneagles Crystal bell with a cut floral decoration. 3.25"dia. x 5.25"h. $65-75.

John Gosnell & Company
Lewes, East Sussex, 1677-

The Gosnell company is primarily a cosmetics producing entity. The Society Belle bell shaped bottle with perfume bottle clapper is a late 19th century item.

A cardboard box for the perfume bell.

A Gosnell bell shaped clear glass with a blue perfume bottle as a clapper. The bell has a molded "Society Belle" and a similar label. 2.75"dia. x 3"h. $75-90.

Mackay & Chisholm
Edinburgh, Scotland, 19th century to mid-20th century

Mackay & Chisholm are noted for their silverware or silverware items attached to glass made by other companies. The silver is usually marked with "M & C" and sometimes with a hallmark of an anchor, lion, and f.
A few glass bells with silver handles are known.

A clear glass bell with small depressions and a silver handle with engraved "M & C" and a hallmark for "Birmingham 1905" 2.25"dia. x 4.4"h. $225-250

Nazeing Glass Works, Ltd.
Broxbourne, Hertfordshire, 1928-

Nazeing Glass Works over the years has produced a variety of glass products, including some ornamental, with bells in later years. Today most of its production is industrial glass with some tableware.

A Nazeing Glass Works clear glass bell with a "Courtney" cut pattern. 3.5"dia. x 7"h. $30-35.

A Nazeing Glass Works clear glass bell with a floral and blue stripe decoration. 3.5"dia. x 6.5"h. $30-35.

Royal Doulton Crystal
Stourbridge

1897 - Thomas Webb and Corbett Ltd., Stourbridge
1906 - Webb Corbett acquires Tutbury Glass Works.
1953 - Company name changed from Thomas Webb and Corbett Ltd to Webb Corbett Ltd.
1969 - Webb Corbett and Tutbury factory acquired by Royal Doulton Company.
1980 - Glassware becomes known as Royal Doulton Crystal by Webb Corbett. The Tutbury Glass Works are closed.
1986 - Webb Corbett name discontinued. Glass marketed as Royal Doulton Crystal.

Most glass bells were made in the 1980s.

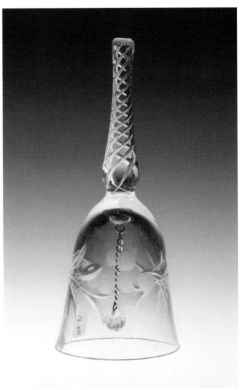

A Royal Doulton clear glass bell with a cut flower decoration and a tapered air twist handle. Signed "Royal Doulton" in a circle. 2.4"dia. x 5.9"h. $35-45.

A Royal Doulton clear glass bell with a cut floral pattern. Made in Slovakia. 3.4"dia. x 5.25"h. $25-30.

Sperrin Crystal
County Tyrone, Northern Ireland, 1984-

Sperrin Crystal is a subsidiary of Glassplax, Inc. of Murrieta, California, and is known for producing cut and etched glass items. At least two cut glass pattern bells are known. Some of its recent glass products have been made in the Czech Republic.

A Sperrin clear crystal bell in the Moyola diamond pattern. 3.25"dia. x 6.6"h. $35-45.

An illustration from a Stevens & Williams 1898 catalog illustrating a cut glass bell.

Stevens & Williams
Brierley Hill, Stourbridge, 1847-1933

A Stevens & Williams glass bell is known to the author and it is their catalog item number 25596, made about 1898. A sketch provided by the Corning Rakow Research Library is shown.

Tudor Crystal Designs, Ltd.

Stourbridge Glass Company, Ltd.
Audnam, Stourbridge, England, 1922-1972

Plowden and Thompson, Ltd.

Dial Glass Works
Stourbridge, England, 1972-

Tudor Crystal was the name used by the Stourbridge Glass Company. It changed its name to Tudor Crystal in 1972. Tudor Crystal is now made by Plowden and Thompson Ltd. Several bells are known with the Tudor label.

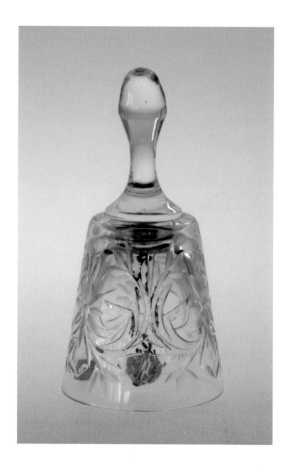

A Tudor Crystal bell with a floral decoration. 1.75"dia. x 3.5"h. $40-45.

Thomas Webb & Company
1840-1855

Thomas Webb & Sons
1859 –

1897- Thomas Webb and Corbett Ltd. established
1906-Webb Corbett acquires Tutbury Glass Works
1920- Joins with Edinburgh and Leith Flint Glass Co. to form Webb's Crystal
       Glass Co. Ltd.
1930s- Thomas Webb and Corbett Ltd. becomes Webb Corbett, Ltd.
1964- Webb's Crystal Glass Co. acquired by Crown House Ltd.
1969- Royal Doulton acquires Webb Corbett, Ltd. and Tutbury Glass Works
1978- Thomas Webb absorbed into the Coloroll Group
1980-Royal Doulton Crystal by Webb Corbett. Tutbury Glass Works closed.
1986-Royal Doulton Crystal. Webb Corbett named discontinued.
1990- The factory is closed.

Several bells labeled Webb are known, but many are labeled with the name of
the company that acquired Webb over the years. For example, see bells shown
under Royal Doulton.

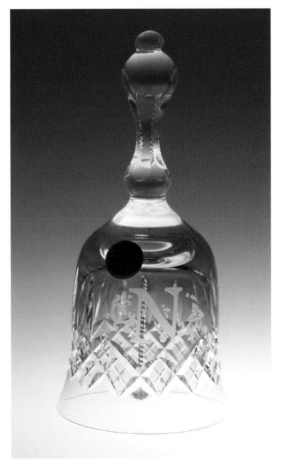

A Webb clear cranberry glass bell with a clear colorless
3 knop handle. 3.5"dia. x 6.5"h. $40-50.

A Webb clear glass bell cut with a crosscut
diamond and miters pattern and etched with a
large "N". 3.4"dia. x 7.25"h. $40-50.

Wedgwood Glass
King's Lynn, Norfolk, 1967-1982

Wedgwood Crystal, Ltd.
1982-1988

Wedgwood Glass and Wedgwood Crystal are names used for articles made by the King's Lynn glassworks after it was acquired by the Wedgwood Group in 1969. Wedgwood became part of Waterford-Wedgwood, PLC in 1986. The Wedgwood Glass operation was closed in 1988.

A Wedgwood Jasper amber glass bell with a white on black cameo of "The Golden Hind' ship. 3"dia. x 6"h. $110-125. The ship, under Sir Francis Drake, circumnavigated the world, 1577-1580.

Two Wedgwood Jasper blue glass bells with white on black cameos of Stubb's Horse. 3.25"dia. x 6"h. $110-125 each.

A Wedgwood clear glass strawberry diamond and fan pattern. Signed "Wedgwood" and made in Yugoslavia. 3"dia. x 7.75"h. $30-35.

Two Wedgwood Jasper amber glass bells with white on black cameos of Stubb's Horse. 3.25"dia. x 5.75"h. $110-125 each.

William Comyns & Sons, Ltd.
London, 1858-1987

Glass bells with applied sterling silver and silver handles are known. They are usually hallmarked with a lion head for London, a standing lion for Sterling, and a WC for William Comyns.

A William Comyns amber glass bell with sterling silver shoulder and handle Hallmarked London 1894. 3.9"dia. x 6.6"h. $400-425. *Courtesy of Sally and Rob Roy.*

English Bells of Unknown Makers

Some bells of unknown maker were made in the United Kingdom, particularly in England. During the 10th century and later, regulations were placed on the size of a drinking vessel. The law required that a 'measure' of ale be marked by a peg on a vessel. The drinker was required to drink to the peg and then pass it on. If a drinker drank beyond the measure he was taking the next drinker "down a peg or two". The peg became a unit of measure. Hence some glass bells were attached to a goblet and marked with pegs.

A clear lavender glass bell with a twisted golden wreath handle and applied hexagonal diamante decoration with pearl center. 1.4"dia. x 3.1"h. $30-40.

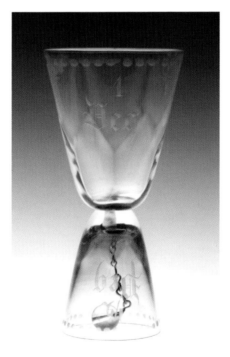

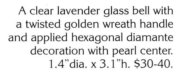

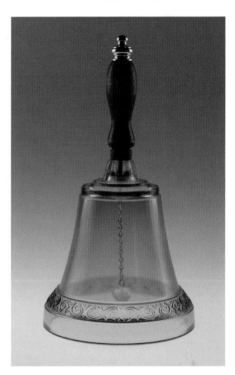

A clear glass bell cut with a diamond pattern, with a metal handle topped by a multifaceted cut crystal. 3"dia. x 5.25"h. $30-35.

A clear glass bell and goblet combined. Marked ½ peg and 1 peg. 2.25"dia. x 4.75"h. $50-60.

An amber glass bell with molded decorated rim and wooden handle. "Made in England" is molded on inside top of glass. 4.5"dia. x 8.5"h. $60-75.

European Bells of Unknown Makers

There are many bells believed to be of European origin, but the country and manufacturer is unknown at this time.

A clear glass bell with diamond and vertical cuts and a hexagonal cut glass handle. 3.75"dia. x 5.4"h. $30-35.

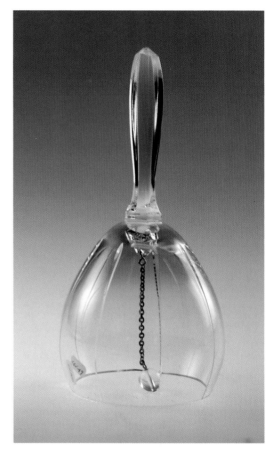

A clear blown glass bell with narrow widely spaced vertical cuts. 3"dia. x 6"h. $30-40.

A clear heavy glass bell with 8 cut facets on the shoulder and cut knob handle. 2.5"dia. x 4"h. $35-45.

A clear cut glass bell with a hobstar, crosscut diamond, and fan pattern and hexagonal pointed handle. 2.4"dia. x 5"h. $30-40.

A clear cut glass bell with a fan and crosscut diamond pattern. 2.5"dia. x 5"h. $100-125.

A clear glass bell with light cutting of berries and a spiral air twist handle. 3.4"dia. x 6.25"h. $20-25.

A clear pressed glass bell in a double line grid and oval pattern. 2.5"dia. x 5.25"h. $15-20.

A clear glass bell with engraved floral decoration. 2"dia. x 3.5"h. $35-45.

A clear glass bell with vertical cuts. 2.9"dia. x 5.1"h. $25-30.

A clear glass bell with pressed diamond pattern. 2.75"dia. x 4.25"h. $15-20.

A heavy clear cut glass bell with a fern wreath design with a center thumbprint together with small diamonds on the rim border. It has a cut octagonal handle with some air bubbles. 6"dia. x 10.25"h. $150-175.

A clear amber glass bell with colorless handle and amber top of knob. 2.6"dia. x 6"h. $20-25.

A Bristol blue glass bell with gold decoration. 3.25"dia. x 5.9"h. $90-100.

A diamond point milk glass bell with short round handle. 2.75"dia. x 3.25"h. $25-30.

An amber blown glass bell with painted flowers and gold trim. 3.9"dia. x 7.9"h. $30-40.

A clear purple glass bell with colorless twisted handle. 3.5"dia. x 7.25"h. $20-25.

A pair of clear blown glass bells with rectangular handles. L. to R. 2.5"dia. x 3.25"h. and 2.4"dia. x 3.1"h. $30-35 each.

Asian Bells

China

Many bells are made in China but the manufacturer is seldom known.

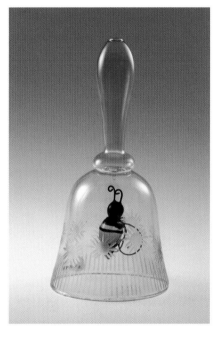

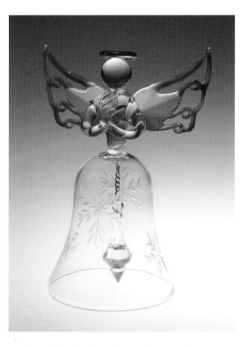

A clear yellow glass bell engraved with flowers and with a bee clapper. Made in China for Department 56, a brand of Lenox Group, Inc. The label shows "Garden Buzz", 2006. 3.25"dia. x 6.9"h. $30-40.

A glass praying angel on a golden glass bell made in China. 1.9"dia. x 4.1"h. $20-25.

A clear glass bell made in China with an angel handle with golden tipped wings and halo and holding a bird in its hands. Several snowflakes are engraved on the bell. 3"dia. x 5.8"h. $30-40.

Three Chinese glass bells with colorful floral handles. Left to right: Iris; daffodil; grape hyacinth. c.2004. 2.75"dia. x 6.5"h. $20-30 each. *Courtesy of Sally and Rob Roy.*

Japan

Kagami Crystal Company, Ltd.
Tokyo, 1934-

The Nippon Sheet Glass Company (NSG) formed Kagami Crystal Works in 1934 to produce and sell crystal glassware and glass handicrafts. It was Japan's first specialized crystal factory. A few bells were produced. In 1937 NSG formed a subsidiary, Nippon Glass.

A Kagami Crystal Co. clear glass bell with a two-knop handle. 2.5"dia. x 3.75"h. $20-25.

A Noritake clear glass bell with a clear green vase handle. 2.25"dia. x 6.75"h. $45-55.

A Noritake clear glass bell with a clear blue glass vase handle. 2.5"dia. x 5"h. $65-75.

Nippon Toki Gomei Kaisha
January 1, 1904

Noritake Co., Inc.
United States, 1947

Noritake Company, Ltd.
Nagoya, 1981-

In 1961 the original company began production of crystal glassware. In 1981 the original company name was changed to Noritake Company Ltd. Subsidiary companies were established all over the world to produce all kinds of products and provide various services. Some glass bells were produced in later years.

Sasaki Glass Company, Ltd.
Tokyo, 1902-1947

Sasaki Glass Company, Inc.
Tokyo, 1947-

The company is the leading glass tableware manufacturer in Japan. Glass bells with gold rims and various handles are well known.

Three Sasaki clear glass bells with gold rim. Left to right: swan handle, 1980, 3.75"dia. x 7.75"h.; ornate handle with flowers, 1981, 3.75"dia. x 7.6"h.; and fan handle, 1982, 3.6"dia. x 3.75"h. $30-40 each.

Taiwan

Many bells have been made in Taiwan, but the companies making them are not usually identified.

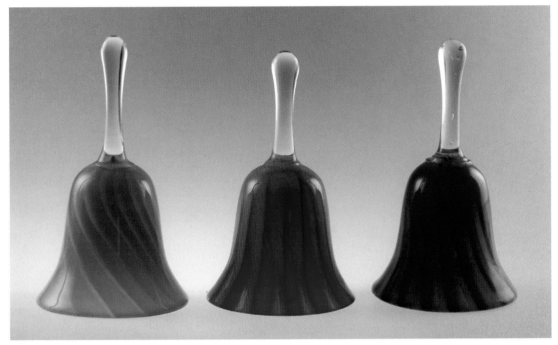

Three glass bells from Taiwan with clear colorless handles. Left to right: light blue, red, and dark blue. c.1976. 3.5"dia. x 6.4"h. $20-25 each.

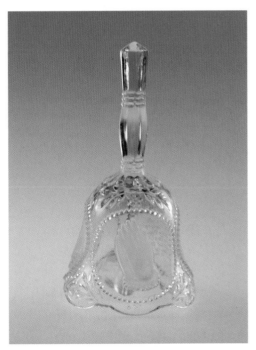

An Emson clear glass bell from Taiwan with a pressed "Lord is my Shepherd". 2.75"dia. x 5.4"h. $15-20.

A clear glass bell with gold rim from Taiwan with a pink rose handle. 3"dia. x 5"h. $25-30.

USSR

An older Russian ruby glass bell is from an unknown manufacturer.

A ruby glass bell with Russian double eagles pattern cut into the glass and gilded. The silver handle is also Russian double eagles and hallmarked "84". 2.9"dia. x 5"h. $150-175. *Courtesy of Sally and Rob Roy.*

Gus-Khrustalny Crystal Factory
Gus-Khrustalny, 1756-

Some recent Russian glass bells can be found with golden dome and cross handles. The cut glass is made in the Gus-Khrustalny Crystal Factory in the city of Gus-Khrustalny, Vladimir province. The golden dome and cross are made in Moscow where they are assembled.

Three Russian cut glass bells with brass orthodox crosses. Left to right: 2.75"dia. x 7"h.; 3"dia. x 5.25"h.; and 2.5"dia. x 7.1"h. All have a label stating "Hand Cut, Gus Khrustalny, Made in Russia". $30-40 each.

Asian Bells of Unknown Makers

Some bells are believed to be of Asian manufacture,
but their maker is unknown.

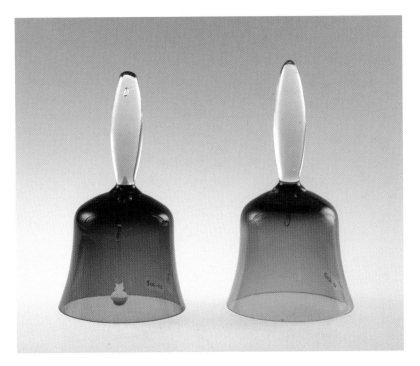

Two clear glass bells: left amethyst bell
with colorless handle, 2.5"dia. x 4.6"h.;
right green bell with colorless handle,
2.5"dia. x 5"h. $15-20 each.

Clear yellow glass and ruby
glass bells with colorless glass
handles. 2.9"dia. x 5.9"h.
c.1974. $15-20 each.

Australian Bells

An end-of-day, two-part blown clear glass bell with 4 knops and a clear brown glass clapper. The bell was made by Alexander Macdonald and William McBean around 1910. 5.6"dia. x 9.1"h. Photo by Marinco Koydanovski. *Courtesy of the Powerhouse Museum, Sydney, NSW, Australia.*

Melbourne Glass Bottle Works

(Also known as Melbourne Glass)
South Melbourne, Victoria, 1872-1915

At the Powerhouse Museum in Sydney, Australia there is a clear blown glass bell together with a walking stick and other glass by the same makers.

South American Bells
Venezuela

ICET Art Murano
Potrerito, Venezuela, 1957-

Bruno Ava went to Venezuela from Italy and in 1957, with some Murano craftsmen, he formed a company to produce Venetian type glass articles. The factory has many furnaces in different stages of glass production. Except for sand, raw materials are imported from Italy. Some glass bells have been produced.

An ICET Art Murano multicolor glass bell with a twisted ring handle. 3.75"dia. x 4.4"h. $50-60.

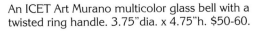

An ICET Art Murano multicolor glass bell with a twisted ring handle. 3.75"dia. x 4.75"h. $50-60.

An ICET Art Murano multicolor glass bell with a twisted clear glass ring handle. 3.2"dia. 4.2"h. $50-60.

Wedding Bells

English Wedding Bells

There are a variety of glass bells blown in two parts and usually joined together by the insertion of the handle into a socket in the top of the bowl of the bell and held together by plaster of paris. The bells are known to bell collectors as wedding bells as the English variety of these bells were often given as wedding presents during the reign of Queen Victoria in the nineteenth century.

A clear cranberry glass bell with clear colorless glass handle with 3 knops. 4"dia. x 8.4"h. $200-250.

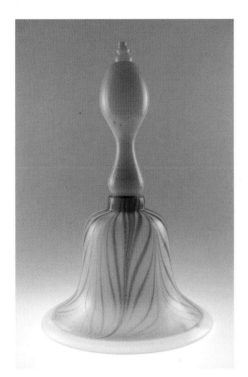

A milk glass bell with irregular pink striping and a milk glass handle with 3 knops. 8.1"dia. x 13.5"h. $1,000-1200.

A milk glass bell with amber Nailsea striping and a one-knop handle. 5.5"dia. x 10"h. $450-500.

A cranberry glass bell with a vaseline glass handle with 3 clear knops. 5.5"dia. x 12.5"h. $475-525.

The following wedding bells are from the collection of Sally and Rob Roy.

A detail of the little girl.

A "Mary Gregory" cranberry glass bell with a decorated little girl and a 4-knop clear colorless glass handle. 6.1"dia. x 12"h. $325-375.

A clear colorless glass bell with pink and blue spots and a 5 knop cranberry glass handle. 5.75"dia. x 13"h. $325-375.

A clear colorless swirled glass bell with a multi-part handle with a bird on the top. 6.1"dia. x 13.5"h. $275-325.

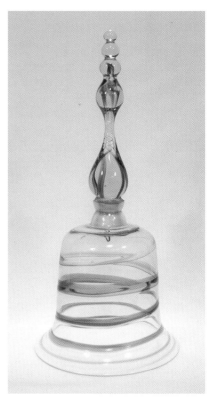

A clear colorless glass bell with violet swirls and a 3-knop handle with pink ribbon. 6"dia. x 13"h. $225-275.

A cranberry on white Nailsea pattern bell with a clear cranberry glass handle with one colorless glass knop. 5"dia. x 9.5"h. $475-525.

A cranberry glass bell with a clear colorless handle with white ribbons topped by a hand. 6.25"dia. x 15"h. $500-600.

A cranberry glass bell with a white rim and a clear colorless handle with Nailsea type white striping and one dark red knop. 4"dia. x 8.1"h. $225-275.

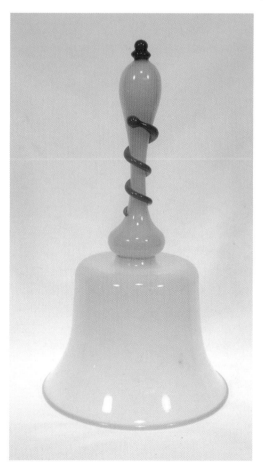

A cream colored glass bell with a blue rim and a handle wrapped with a blue snake and topped by a blue knop. 6.75"dia. x 8.5"h. $600-650.

A clear colorless glass bell with pink and blue swirls and spots and a 4 knop handle. 5.4"dia. x 11.1"h. $225-275.-

A clear colorless glass bell with white Nailsea striping and a clear green glass 3-knop handle. 2.75"dia. x 5.6"h. $350-400.

Two yellow glass bells. The left bell has a yellow glass 4-knop handle. 3"dia. x 6.4"h. $350-375. The bell on the right has a colorless 3-knop handle and a colorless clapper. 2.9"dia. x 7.4"h. $200-250.

Two cranberry glass bells with colorless handles. left to right: twisted 2-knop handle. 3.9"dia. x 6"h.; 3-knop handle. 3"dia. x 6.25"h. $200-250 each.

A clear glass bell with yellow striping and a solid yellow glass 3-knop handle. 2.75"dia. x 5.6"h. $350-400.

A turquoise glass bell with white Nailsea striping and a clear turquoise 4-knop handle. 3.75"dia. x 7.75"h. $450-475.

A cranberry glass bell with white Nailsea striping and a clear blue glass handle with 5 opalescent vaseline glass knops. 4.75"dia. x 10"h. $425-475.

A white glass bell with mottled red spots and a green rim. The handle is clear dark green glass with 4 knops. 5"dia. x 10"h. $425-475.

Butler Institute of American Art

The Butler Institute of American Art, Youngstown, Ohio, has a collection of glass wedding bells donated to the Institute by a bell collector, Fanniebelle McVey Trippe. The Institute has granted permission to publish photographs of this large collection of about 100 bells. The photographs were taken by Marinco Koydanovski.

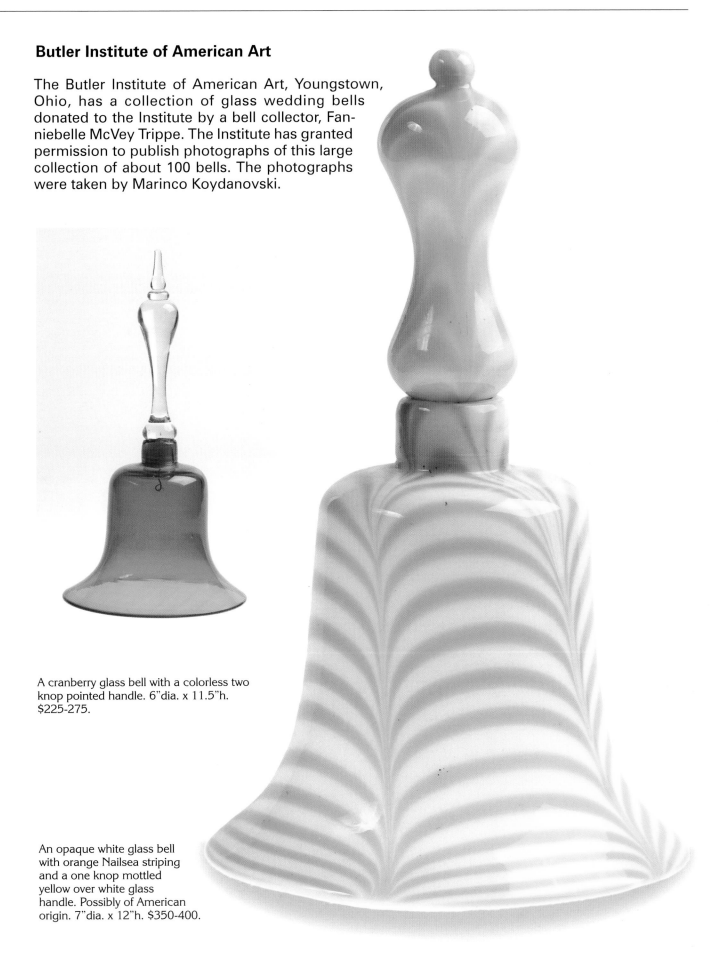

A cranberry glass bell with a colorless two knop pointed handle. 6"dia. x 11.5"h. $225-275.

An opaque white glass bell with orange Nailsea striping and a one knop mottled yellow over white glass handle. Possibly of American origin. 7"dia. x 12"h. $350-400.

An opaque white glass bell with ruffled rim. 5.25"dia. x 10"h. $200-250.

A clam broth colored bell with dark handle. 5.5"dia. x 9.5"h. $200-250.

An opalescent white glass smoke bell. 7.25"dia. x 9"h. $200-225.

A clear glass bell with gold colored
handle and clear colorless one knop.
3.5"dia. x 9.5"h. $200-300.

A smoky swirled blue glass bell with milk glass handle.
4.5"dia. x 8.25"h. $200-250.

A clear colorless glass bell with a one-knop
handle. 4.5"dia. x 9.75"h. $200-250.

A colorless bell with black rim and socket and brown three knop handle. 4"dia. x 10"h. $250-300.

A turquoise glass bell with amber handle with three knops. 4.75"dia. x 11"h. $250-300.

A colorless glass bell with Nailsea loops and three-knop handle. 4.75"dia. x 10"h. $275-325.

A cranberry glass bell with a colorless, four-knop handle. 5.5"dia. x 11.5"h. $275-325.

A dark blue glass bell with a milk glass one-knop handle. 4"dia. x 9"h. $200-250.

An aqua colored glass bell with milk glass handle. 4.5"dia. x 8"h. $225-275.

A diamond cranberry glass bell with cream colored two-knop handle. 6.5"dia. x 12.5"h. $300-375.

A quilted cranberry glass bell with gold decoration over clear colorless glass two-knop handle. 6.6"dia. x 11.5"h. $350-400.

A diamond quilted cranberry glass bell with a clear blue, two-knop handle. 6.5"dia. x 10.5"h. $300-375.

A clear blue glass bell with colorless, four-knop handle. 5"dia. x 11.75"h. $275-325.

A swirled cranberry glass bell with a swirled colorless, two-knop handle. 7"dia. x 11.25"h. $250-300.

A clear glass bell with white Nailsea striping. 5"dia. x 12"h. $300-350.

A swirled cranberry glass bell with a colorless two-knop handle. 7"dia. x 11.5"d. $250-300.

A cranberry glass bell with a colorless, two-knop, pointed handle. 5.5"dia. x 11.5"h. $225-275.

A clear colorless bell with greenish ribbed glass base and ruby colored handle. 3"dia. x 5.25"h. $150-200.

An amber glass bell with an opaque white, one-knop handle. 8"dia. x 18"h.
$300-375.

A rose colored glass bell with a swirled colorless handle.
6.5"dia. x 10.5"h. $225-275.

A cranberry glass bell with a
swirled colorless glass handle.
6.5"dia. x 13.5"h. $$250-300.

A cobalt blue glass bell with three golden ribs along the rim and a golden handle with one golden knop and two clear colorless knops. 5.5"dia. x 12.5"h. $300-400.

A clear glass bell with Nailsea white looping and a clear dark pointed amber handle with two knops. 4.25"dia. x 9.75"h. $250-300.

An opalescent cranberry hobnail glass bell with a light blue, two-knop handle. Possibly of American origin. 7"dia. x 12.5"h. $300-400.

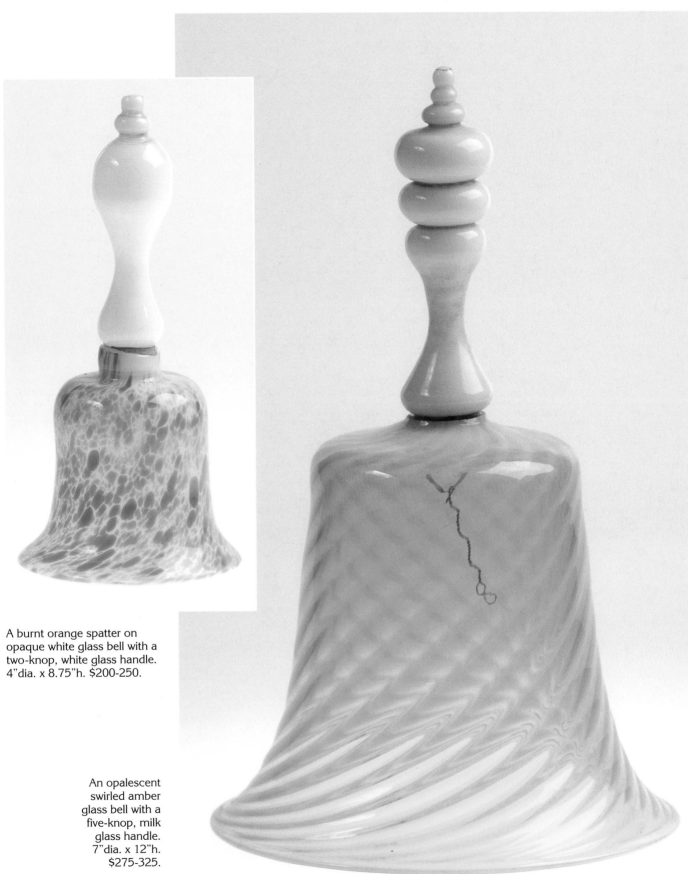

A burnt orange spatter on opaque white glass bell with a two-knop, white glass handle. 4"dia. x 8.75"h. $200-250.

An opalescent swirled amber glass bell with a five-knop, milk glass handle. 7"dia. x 12"h. $275-325.

A pink spatter over opaque white glass bell with white, two-knop handle. 4.75"dia. x 10"h. $250-300.

A pigeon blood and blue end-of-day glass bell with a three-knop milk white handle. 4.75"dia. x 10.5"h. $275-325.

A cranberry glass bell with white rim and clear colorless handle with three dark green knops. 6.5"dia. x 13.5"h. $275-325.

An opaque white and rose, Nailsea swirl, glass bell with a blue rim and opaque white, one-knop handle. 6"dia. x 10.5"h. $300-400.

A vaseline opalescent, swirl glass bell with a six-knop, clear colorless glass handle. 5"dia. x 11"h. $275-325.

An amber glass bell with white rim and clear colorless, one-knop handle. 5.5"dia. x 11.25"h. $250-300.

A turquoise blue glass bell with an opaque cream band along the rim and a colorless handle with three blue knops. 5.25"dia. x 13.25"h. $300-375.

A clear colorless glass bell with white Nailsea type swirls with a clear handle with four knops. 5.5"dia. x 12"h. $300-400.

A cobalt blue, glass bell with a clear colorless, swirled and pointed glass handle. 4.5"dia. x 11.5"h. $300-400.

A clear cranberry, swirled glass bell with a custard rim and three-knop, custard handle. 6"dia. x 12.5"h. $300-400.

A quilted, honey amber, clear glass bell with an opaque white handle. 4.5"dia. x 9"h. $200-275.

A deep turquoise glass bell with a swirled base and an opaque white handle with a turquoise knop. 6"dia. x 11"h. $300-400.

An opaque white glass bell with a deep ruby glass rim and a clear colorless, three-knop handle. 5"dia. x 9"h. $250-300.

A quilted diamond raspberry glass bell with a twisted clear colorless handle with four knops. 7"dia. x 13.5"h. $300-400.

A clear cranberry glass bell with an opaque white rim and clear colorless handle with white Nailsea swirls and three knops. 6.5"dia. x 14.5"h. $300-375.

A clear glass bell with blue, red, and white speckles and a clear colorless glass handle with two blue knops. 5.75"dia. x 12.5"h. $300-400.

A clear, cobalt-blue, glass bell with a clear colorless, one-knop handle. 7"dia. x 12"h. $250-300.

A clear cranberry glass bell with a white rim and a clear colorless glass handle with white Nailsea loops and topped by a hand. 5.75"dia. x 13"h. $375-450.

A cranberry swirled glass bell with an amber swirled glass handle with three knops. 5.25"dia. x 11.75"h. $350-400.

An aqua clear glass bell with a milk glass handle with one dark blue knop. 5.25"dia. x 11.25"h. $300-350.

An aqua clear glass bell with a milk glass handle with two dark blue knops. 5.4"dia. x 11"h. $300-350.

A cranberry swirled glass bell with an opaque white glass, four-knop handle. 6.25"dia. x 11.5"h. $325-375.

A turquoise diamond quilted glass bell with blue spatter and an opaque white, two-knop handle. 6"dia. x 11"h. $300-375.

A clear cranberry glass bell with three-ribbed rim and a golden glass, three-knop handle. 6.5"dia. x 13"h. $325-375.

A honey amber, clear glass bell with a colorless glass, three-knop handle. 5.5"dia. x 11.5"h. $300-350.

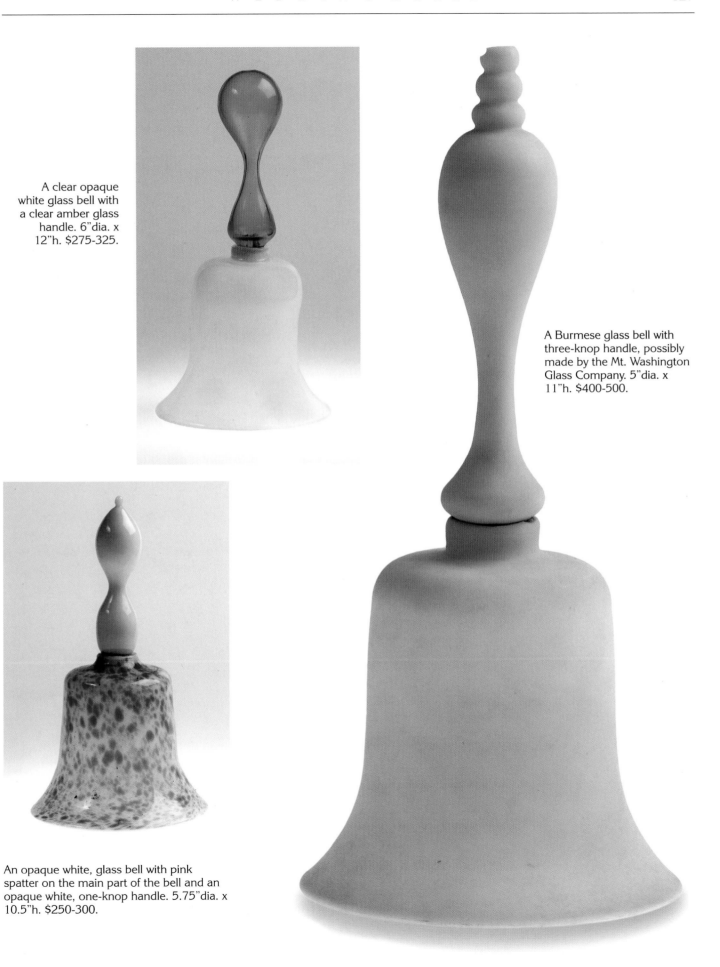

A clear opaque white glass bell with a clear amber glass handle. 6"dia. x 12"h. $275-325.

A Burmese glass bell with three-knop handle, possibly made by the Mt. Washington Glass Company. 5"dia. x 11"h. $400-500.

An opaque white, glass bell with pink spatter on the main part of the bell and an opaque white, one-knop handle. 5.75"dia. x 10.5"h. $250-300.

A cobalt blue, glass bell with white Nailsea striping and a clear red glass handle. Some knops are missing. 5.25"dia. x 11.5"h. $250-300.

A clear blue, glass bell with an opaque white, one-knop handle. 5.25"dia. x 12.25"h. $250-325.

A cranberry glass bell with a clear, three-knop handle with a red, white, and blue spiral. 4.5"dia. x 11"h. $450-500.

A clear glass bell with interior decorated with cigar labels.
Made for an American cigar manufacturer for display in one
of their offices. 6.25"dia. x 11"h. $500-600.

Another view of the 4.5"dia. x 9"h. bell with cigar labels.

Another American clear glass bell with interior decorated with cigar labels. 4.5" dia. x 9"h. $300-400.

An opaque white glass bell with a blue ruffled rim and black handle. 4.5"dia. x 9.5"h. $300-350.

A cranberry glass bell with a spiral bronze handle. 5"dia. x 10"h. $300-400.

A blue glass bell with a pink and white, one-knop handle. 4"dia. x 7.25"h. $250-300.

A pigeon blood, glass bell with a diamond quilted pattern and a one-knop handle. 5.75"dia. x 11"h. $300-400.

A clear smoke, glass bell.
6"dia. x 7"h. $175-225.

A swirled, amber, glass bell
with a clear colorless, ribbed
handle with four knops.
4"dia. x 9.25"h. $275-325.

A cobalt blue, glass bell with an opaque white, two-knop handle. 6"dia. x 11.25"h. $275-325.

A cobalt blue, glass bell with an opaque white, two-knop handle. 4.75"dia. x 10.25"h. $275-325.

A deep amber, glass bell with a clear colorless, two-knop pointed handle. 5.75"dia. x 12.25"h. $275-325.

An aqua glass bell with ruffled rim and an opaque white glass handle with three knops. 5.5"dia. x 12"h. $300-325.

A light amber, glass bell with a clear colorless, two-knop handle. 5"dia. x 12"h. $275-325.

A cranberry glass bell with a colorless, five-knop handle. 5.75"dia. x 12.75"h. $300-325.

A swirled, cranberry glass bell with a colorless, swirled glass, three-knop handle. 5"dia. x 12.5"h. $300-350.

A swirled, cranberry glass bell with a colorless, swirled glass, four-knop handle. 5"dia. x 13.75"h. $300-350.

A ruby glass bell with ruffled rim and an opaque white handle. 5"dia. x 9"h. $225-275.

A cranberry glass bell with a
colorless, two-knop handle.
7"dia. x 14"h. $275-325.

A cranberry glass bell with a
colorless, four-knop handle.
4.75"dia. x 11.25"h. $250-300.

A cranberry glass bell with a colorless, three knop handle. 4.5"dia. x 10"h. $250-300.

A cranberry glass bell with a colorless, four-knop handle. 5.5"dia. x 13.5"h. $250-300.

A cranberry glass bell with a colorless, four-knop handle. 6"dia. x 13"h. $250-300.

A cranberry glass bell with a colorless, six-knop handle. 5.25"dia. x 11.75"h. $250-300.

A cranberry glass bell with a colorless, three-knop handle. 5"dia. x 11.5"h. $250-300.

A cranberry glass bell with a colorless, three-knop handle. 4.75"dia. x 10.75"h. $225-275.

A deep amber, glass bell with a colorless, four-knop handle attached to the bell with a brass fitting. 5"dia. x 11.75"h. $275-325.

An opaque blue, glass bell with an opaque white handle and white and blue knops. 6"dia. x 11.25"h. $275-325.

An end-of-day, opaque white, glass bell with red, yellow, and blue spatter and an opaque white, one-knop handle. Possibly American. 6.25"dia. x 10.5"h. $300-400.

A cranberry, swirl glass bell with an opaque white, three-knop handle. 5.75"dia. x 11.75"h. $325-400.

A cobalt blue, glass bell with a colorless, one-knop handle attached to the bell with a brass ring. 5.25"dia. x 9"h. 275-325.

A coffee-colored, glass bell with painted floral decoration and an opaque white, three-knop handle. 5.25"dia. x 10"h. $400-500.

A cranberry glass bell with a colorless, twisted handle with five knops. 6"dia. x 14"h. $350-400.

A light amber, glass bell with an opaque white handle. 5.5"dia. x 10.5"h. $250-300.

An opaque white glass bell with blue, aqua, and pink spatters and an opaque white handle. 5"dia. x 10"h. $275-325.

A cranberry glass bell with a double-lip rim and three-knop, mercury-glass handle. 5"dia. x 12"h. $350-425.

A cranberry glass bell with a colorless, four-knop handle. 4.5"dia. x 11"h. $275-325.

The following wedding bells are from the collection of Marilyn Grismere. Photos by Pete Bender.

A red, swirl glass bell with cream- colored, hollow handle and three vaseline knops. 5.9"dia. x 11.5"h. $300-350.

A clear glass bell with white Nailsea striping. Clear handle with dimpled effect. 5.1"dia. x 10.25"h. $250-300.

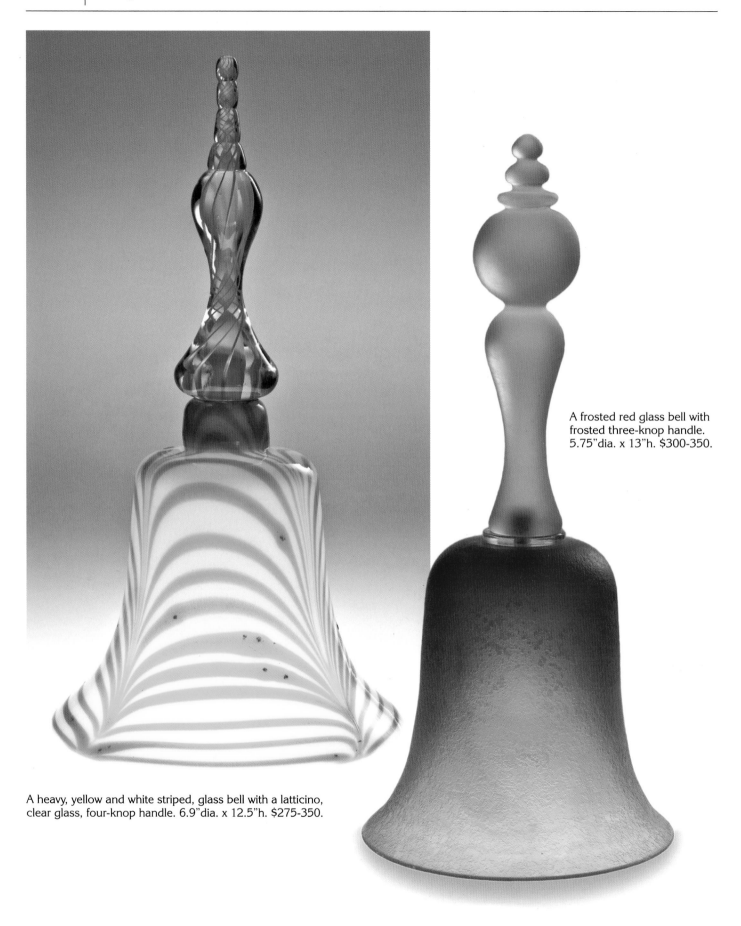

A heavy, yellow and white striped, glass bell with a latticino, clear glass, four-knop handle. 6.9"dia. x 12.5"h. $275-350.

A frosted red glass bell with frosted three-knop handle. 5.75"dia. x 13"h. $300-350.

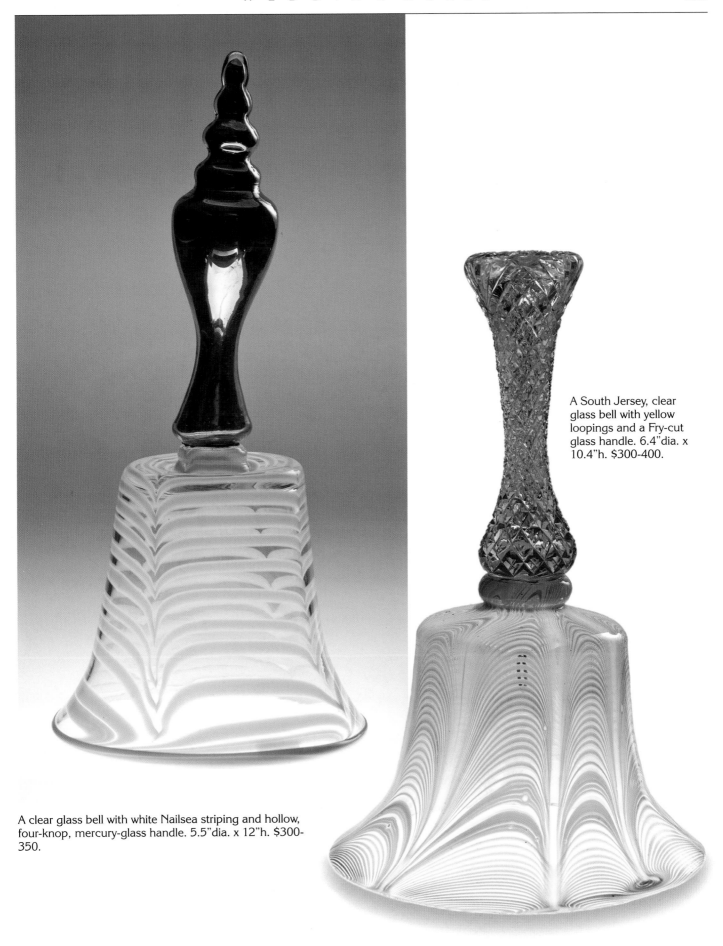

A South Jersey, clear glass bell with yellow loopings and a Fry-cut glass handle. 6.4"dia. x 10.4"h. $300-400.

A clear glass bell with white Nailsea striping and hollow, four-knop, mercury-glass handle. 5.5"dia. x 12"h. $300-350.

A red, swirled glass bell with a white rim and colorless, latticino, four-knop handle. 5.75"dia. x 12"h. $275-325.

A rose colored glass bell with air bubbles and a clear green, three-knop handle. 4.9"dia. x 11.4"h. $250-300.

A green glass bell with painted roses and white, one-knop handle. Attributed to the Phoenix Glass Company. 7.4"dia. x 10.9"h. $400-500.

A pink, swirled glass bell with a yellow, two-knop handle joined to the base with a brass ring. 6.25"dia. x 10.5"h. $250-275.

A clear purple glass bell with a five-knop, clear glass handle with blue and purple ribbon. 6.6"dia. x 13.5"h. $250-300.

A lavender glass bell with white Nailsea striping and a one-knop, clear glass handle with white and rose ribbons. 5.1"dia. x 11.25"h. $250-300.

A clear red, glass bell with a clear colorless handle topped with a white glass hand. 6.25"dia. x 12.1"h. $350-450.

A red, clear glass, diamond pattern bell with a white. one-knop handle. 5.75"dia. x 11"h. $300-350.

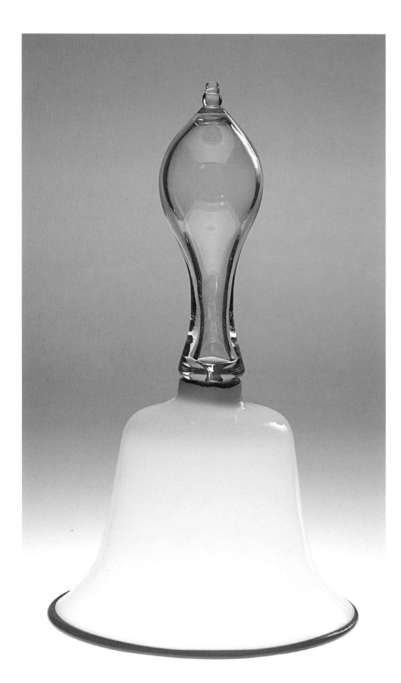

A milk glass bell with brown rim and a clear glass, two-knop handle. 6"dia. x 10.25"h. $250-300.

A heavy clear red glass bell with a hollow clear colorless five-knop handle. 6.5"dia. x 11.9"h. $300-325.

◆ ◆ ◆ ◆ ◆ ◆ ◆ ◆ ◆ ◆ ◆ ◆ ◆ ◆

The American Bell Association

The American Bell Association (ABA), is an international association of bell collectors. It was formed originally in 1940 as the National Bell Collectors Club. The name was changed in 1948 to the American Bell Association; and in 1984, the word International was added to reflect a growing international membership and was incorporated as a non-profit organization.

The association has 39 regional, state, Canadian and overseas chapters that meet on a regular basis. It holds an annual convention during June/July and publishes a bimonthly magazine, The Bell Tower, featuring articles by members on all kinds of bells, world bell news, chapter news, and details of important future bell meetings.

Conventions are held in a different location each year and they afford members the opportunity to become acquainted with other members and their collections as well as forging lasting friendships. Highlights of each convention are bell programs, a sales room, and a bell auction with many opportunities to find bells to add to members' collections.

For further information, write to:
American Bell Association International, Inc.
7210 Bellbrook Drive
San Antonio, TX 78227-1002

Index ◆ ◆ ◆ ◆ ◆ ◆ ◆ ◆ ◆ ◆ ◆ ◆ ◆ ◆

Air twist handle 68-70, 75, 81
Alfred Taub, Vohenstrasse, Gmbh 47
Angel 62, 85
Atlantis, S.A. 64
Bell & goblet 79
Bull Fight 43
Burns Crystal Company 70
Caithness Glass, Ltd. 70
Cavan Crystal Designs Ltd. 50
Chalet Artistic Glass, Ltd. 11
Christallerie Daum 43
Christalleries Royales
    de Champagne 42
Christmas 18
cigar labels 130, 131
clown 56, 59
Crisa 57, 58
Dartington Crystal, Ltd. 71
Dartington Glass 71
Demaine Glass Studio 12
Dial Glass Works 76
Dresden Crystal 48
devil 43
Edinburgh and Leith Flint Glass
    Company, The 72
Edinburgh Crystal Glass
    Company, The 72
Ekenas Glasbruk 68
Emson 87
Failte Crystal 50
Galactic Art Glass Studio, Inc. 13
Galway Irish Crystal Ltd. 50
Glass
    Burmese 53, 127
    Cranberry 31, 97, 107-148
    Diamond quilted 107
    Filigree 13-28
    Flint 43
    Gilded 38, 40, 44, 69, 82, 86, 88, 126
    Multilayer 34, 36, 48, 53
    Murano 52, 56, 58-62, 93
    Nailsea 58, 97-101, 105, 108, 112,
    116, 118, 121, 123, 128, 151, 153, 156
    Opaline 44

Ribbon 13-28, 30
    Vaseline 100
Gleneagles Crystal Company, Ltd. 72
Gleneagles of Edinburgh, Ltd. 72
Goebel, House of 45
Golden Hind 78
Graf Schaffgottsch'sche
    Josephinenhutte 45
Gus-Khrustalny Crystal Factory 88
Hadeland Glassverk A/S 63
Holmegaard Glassworks 41
Honi soit qui mal y pense 43
House of Goebel 45
ICET Art Muano 93
James Deakin 71
James Deakin & Sons 71
James Deakin & Sons Ltd. 71
Jenny Kravits 51
John Gosnell & Company 73
Kagami Crystal Company, Ltd. 86
Krosno S.A. 63
Lausitzer Glashuette, AG 48
Loch Lomond 70
London 78
Macdonald, Alexander 91
Mackay & Chisholm 73
Mantorp Glasbruk AB 68
Mary Gregory 96
McBean, William 91
Melbourne Glass 91
Melbourne Glass Bottle Works 91
Mt. Washington Glass Company 127
Murano 52, 56, 58-62, 93
Nailsea 58, 97-101, 105, 108, 112, 116,
    118, 121, 123, 128, 151, 153, 156
Napoleon 42-44
Nazeing Glass Works, Ltd. 74
Neptune 71
Nippon Toki Gomei Kaisha 86
Noritake Co., Inc. 86
Noritake Company, Ltd. 86
Orrefors Glasbruk 68, 69
Palda Glas 33
Phoenix Glass Company 155

Plowden and Thompson, Ltd. 76
Powerhouse Museum 91
Robert Held Art Glass 30
Rogaska Glassverk 66
Rossi Glass Inc. 31
Royal Doulton Crystal 75
Ruckl, Antonin 40
Ruckl Crystal 40
Sasaki Glass Company, Inc. 86
Sasaki Glass Company, Ltd. 86
Sir Francis Drake 78
Smoke bell 102, 134
Snookum Art Glass, Inc. 30
Society Belle 73
Sperrin Vrystal 76
Stevens & Williams 76
Stourbridge Glass Company, Ltd. 76
Stubb's Horse 78
Thomas Webb & Company 77
Thomas Webb & Sons 77
Tudor Crystal Designs, Ltd. 76
Tuscany 55
Val St. Lambert 34
Vase handle 86
Venus de Milo 42
Vidrios de Arte Gordiola, S. L. 67
Wedgwood Crystal, Ltd. 78
Wedgwood Glass 78
William Comyns & Sons, Ltd. 78